LEADERSHIP BEYOND GOOD INTENTIONS

What it takes to really make a difference

GEOFF AIGNER

ALLEN&UNWIN

To May

First published in Australia in 2011

Allen & Unwin
83 Alexander Street
Crows Nest NSW 2065
Australia
Phone: (61 2) 8425 0100
Fax: (61 2) 9906 2218
Email: info@allenandunwin.com
Web: www.allenandunwin.com

Cataloguing-in-Publication details are available from the National Library of Australia
www.trove.nla.gov.au

978 1 74237 394 2

Typeset in 11/15 Minion by Midland Typesetters, Australia
Printed and bound in Australia by the SOS Print + Media Group.

10 9 8 7 6 5 4 3

The paper in this book is FSC® certified. FSC® promotes environmentally responsible, socially beneficial and economically viable management of the world's forests.

Contents

Foreword

An often underestimated richness in life today and in realms of science is the vast amount of information that may be immediately accessed and combined, adding ever new dimensions to beings' search for meaning and happiness and to those who wish to avoid getting stuck in unproductive and often boring loops of activity.

Building on many years of experience, and with a keen sense of social responsibility, my friend Geoff shares his suggestions on a caring society for leaders from business, government, and the social and private sectors.

Comparing and combining the solutions and experiences given over thousands of years by humanistic cultures and religions with the latest of today's practical and statistical knowledge, I see a powerful and convincing force for good appearing with this book. May it benefit many.

Lama Ole Nydahl

Acknowledgements

The stories and people discussed in this book are real. I would like to thank those who have shared their experiences and ideas with me. These include Tania Adams, Jeff Cheverton, Jennifer Cullen, Kyrstie Dunn, Dominic Grenot, Sheila Matete-Owiti, Richard Matthews, Liz Skelton, Jude Stoddart, Nicole Yade and Mark Yettica-Paulson.

I would also like to thank the people who read all or parts of the manuscript and gave me very useful feedback, which not only helped the book but also my growth in the process: my wife May, who was both patient, caring and challenging; my colleagues and friends at Social Leadership Australia, Liz Skelton and Robbie Macpherson, provided invaluable encouragement and insight. Rosamund Christie and Adam Kahane generously offered their time and feedback in reading the manuscript.

There are others who have taught, helped or encouraged along the way. Foremost is Ole Nydahl. Also, Sarah Maddison, Maike Brill, Rob Sok and Katrina Hosie.

The consulting and leadership development work of Social Leadership Australia (SLA) has provided the basis for many of the ideas in this book. SLA is a part of The Benevolent Society, Australia's oldest charity, established in 1813 as an independent, not-for-profit, non-religious organisation. SLA was established in 1999 to generate lasting positive social impact by creating a network of civic leaders from all sectors: corporate, government and community. I would like to acknowledge The Benevolent Society and its support in allowing this book to come to life.

Introduction and overview

GOOD INTENTIONS ARE NOT ENOUGH

It is often surprising for people who want to make positive change in their organisations or communities to find themselves facing much resistance and many obstacles. These difficulties are not unique to any particular sector, community, profession or culture. It is not uncommon for:

- managers in corporations fighting for the sustainability of their business to themselves get scape-goated;
- social workers dealing with marginalised communities to feel they have run out of compassion;
- social activists with an important message to get sidelined, ridiculed or not even heard;
- spiritual leaders charged with the development of their congregations to get stymied by the conflicting expectations they face;

- public servants shouldered with our most difficult problems to become cynical and lose hope.

The temptation is to look outside ourselves to answer these problems, to look to new tools, frameworks or models. We see problems in our environment. We may find that the individuals or institutions we are working with are wilfully or ignorantly blocking change. The timing might be wrong. These are all important factors, but we may not be looking at one of the most important parts of the challenges we face: ourselves. It can be hard for us to admit that we might be part of the problem we are trying to fix. It is usually easier to give up, than to see our own role in the mess. After all, we often put our heart and soul into what we are doing. Moreover, we may receive (at least when we start) many positive affirmations from friends and colleagues on how important our work is and why we need to keep doing it.

This book looks at why, despite there being so many skilled, willing and dedicated change agents with good intentions, we still face intractable problems. Its focus is you. Let me explain by way of a story:

It's March 2008 and I am somewhere outside of Broome in north-west Australia in a 4WD bus with a group of 30 people. Outside, the brilliant red sand of the Kimberleys shimmers in the unforgiving midday sun. The heat is intense.

I left Sydney 18 hours ago excited to be part of the first 'Australian Dialogue', a process to begin a new conversation between black and white Australians. On the plane I spent most of the time diligently (and I admit anxiously) reading all the background material. On arrival into Broome, I shook hands eagerly with the other participants.

Now, 30 minutes later, I am sitting at the back of the bus with a group of people I already feel quite distant from, not knowing where we are going, not understanding why we are driving north instead of south (I read the map incorrectly!), feeling more and more nauseous as we hit big bumps at seemingly faster speeds. And inevitably I wonder what I am doing here and whether this really was such a good idea.

And then it struck me! This is what happens to so many of us. We start with good intentions and excitement and then find ourselves in the middle of nowhere, not knowing where we are going or why, and unsure about our company. And we generally have a set of fixed responses—we can take it out on our fellow travellers, look for a new bus, keep on travelling into the desert and oblivion, or turn around and go home.

I wanted to go home.

If we are honest with ourselves we know that the problem is not just the bus or our colleagues and the answer may be something other than turning around or continuing on. In a way the environment is irrelevant because sooner or later we are going to find ourselves in the same predicament again. And I know I will feel the urge to go home, like I did at that moment. I will also probably find all the usual (and very convincing) reasons to do exactly that.

These moments when we hit our edges are critical points in determining how effective we can be as social leaders. They signal an opportunity to look more deeply. Instead, we usually end up turning to quick fixes, making hasty judgements, fleeing and scape-goating. We need to understand what it is that is resonating for us when we end up 'on the bus in the desert' and what might be a useful way out of it.

BEYOND GOOD INTENTIONS

This book is for people who have hope and good intentions, but have faced the reality of making change. People who may not want to change the world, but think their part of it could be better—maybe a lot better.

Leadership is about making ourselves useful. To our organisations, our community, our families, the world. Being useful means ensuring things are better than we found them, not giving short-term, feel-good responses and leaving the problems for someone else to fix. Or hoping they go away. It is a privilege to be able to attempt this kind of work. The world needs this kind of leadership; leadership that can transcend our egos and bring love, freedom and compassion to those we work with and for.

But if we are working on being useful and making things better, there comes a time in our development when we need to look at ourselves and how we are operating. We can't rely on policy, government, project plans, committees, movements and ideology. Ultimately we come back to the things we can control—ourselves. This is the basic premise of this book: that individuals are responsible for initiating and implementing change. In the end, it is individuals and groups of individuals who have made change happen in the world. We can't pretend that we are not important. Yet strangely (and understandably), we tend to look externally for solutions and not at how we are operating. That's because it's hard and at times uncomfortable work to see ourselves as part of the problem—it's hard to learn.

We may say we are interested in learning, but usually we only mean that on our terms. And this is why we see so little useful leadership in our world, because while we may desire change and progress, leaders are usually unwilling to do this themselves.

But it's not all about making progress outside ourselves: understanding and doing something about how we work is useful not only for the problems we face and the people we are working with, but also (and maybe most importantly) it is useful for us. I am always surprised by how difficult it is for some leaders I have worked with to talk about what they are personally getting out of their efforts to make progress. Are we happier? In good health? Learning? Wiser? Or are we just 'busy'?

That makes this book about practice, not theory, written for people who are 'in it'—working on a change, reflecting on what it would take to start or even recovering after the last attempt. It is a book for people who want to find new and more useful ways to lead for themselves and their organisation or community. People like you and me who have had a go, had some successes and some failures and want to move to another level in how we are operating. They may feel hopeful, but might also have a niggling feeling that all their great attempts are starting to feel tired and that to take the next big leap, something fundamental needs to shift.

WHAT'S REQUIRED?

The kind of shifts this book explores starts with looking at some of the inner tensions involved in making change and challenging some of the assumptions about ourselves, our motivations and methods.

To do that, it aims to fill a gap between two very different fields. The first is the large field of leadership and change theory. The second field is what I will call the inner journey. In the bookshops you will find this in the section called 'spiritual' or 'self-development'. Leadership and the inner journey seem not to intersect. We forget the great inner journeys that all of the leaders who inspire us took through their lives. Maybe it is easier to focus on the mythical stories and the 'how to's' than on the reality of making change.

Yet, the external leadership challenges we face and the inner journey we undertake are inextricably linked. Our failure to bring these two paths together is, in my experience, the biggest stumbling block for experienced change practitioners. This is the critical intersection point between ourselves and the work we have to do.

This book has three sections that reflect what I think are the essential elements in building our capacity to exercise leadership. The first is understanding the system. SWOT analyses and market, staff and client surveys are all great background reading. More important is examining the *fundamental human dynamics* that play out every time we enter a system and try to take action. There has been much written about how systems react to change, but not the *needs* that are being filled by these reactions. There has also been surprisingly little written on how we are part of what's going on (part of the mess) rather than being wholly objective, neutral and independent beings.

Which leads to the second section: understanding ourselves. This goes beyond the usual self-awareness tools and personal inventories that most of us are already familiar with, to look at the personal questions that usually arise in making change. These may not be things you would expect to find. For example, how can our ideas of compassion, as good as they may sound, actually be getting in the way of progress? How does our judgement help us? Is it useful or limiting? Can judgement really help at all? Why does leading change fill me with fear or completely exhaust me? What does it look like when I am trying to exercise leadership—is it joyous or onerous—and is it inspiring for others to follow in our footsteps? These are important questions that can often trip up experienced change leaders.

Finally, the third section looks at what it means to work with others. Leadership, by definition, is not a solo sport. The issues we are working with cannot be solved on our own: they require collaboration. Working with others, particularly those who don't share our views, raises difficult questions of politics, values and authenticity.

The process of learning that this book promotes works best with practice. It works best accompanied by collaboration with others and self-reflection. Some reflection exercises and meditations to support the ideas have been included.

PROMOTING A NEW IDEA OF LEADERSHIP

The kind of change described in this book is not so much about values as about an ideal. It focuses on us as people who want to make positive change. That's the kind of change where we can start to understand and solve our own problems, meaning we are in a better place than where we started.

In our work at Social Leadership Australia at The Benevolent Society we use the words 'social leadership' or 'civic leadership' to reinforce the idea that leadership is about working for and with others—it is a *world* view, a view that looks beyond ourselves. The words social and civic do not imply it is more useful to people from the community sector than those from the corporate sector. It is a reminder that all leadership is a social experience as it involves people and understanding and working with who they are. It is meant to wake us up to the reality of leadership as a social exercise— wherever we work—and that ultimately good leadership leads to a more civil society.

The practices and ideas used here come from a number of different sources. Firstly, they are drawn from our experiences at Social Leadership Australia. Over the last decade we have worked with a great many people trying to make progress in their own areas from counter-terrorism police to refugee workers, from Muslim youth to senior bankers, from human rights workers to church elders. We have found that while their circumstances and issues might be different, they all face very similar personal development challenges. Sometimes when working with a group of young people in a marginalised community, I close my eyes and hear the same conversations that take place in a corporate boardroom.

This book draws on my experiences working with many highly motivated, skilled and inspiring people: true learners. I am grateful to have been able to learn from them and also grateful that I may have been able to pay that back as a teacher in more recent years.

Finally, I draw on my own development and learning in exercising leadership—the successes and the failures. All the development areas in this book I have either struggled with myself or continue to work on.

REASONS TO HOPE

The more we advance as human beings, the more we find there are still so many things to do. Sometimes it seems fundamental improvements in education, health care, child abuse, violence in the family, care for our environment and the behaviour of our corporations are out of reach. At a deeper and more personal level we yearn for more—the ability to reach our potential and for those around us to reach theirs. This challenge, humans reaching their full potential, seems harder still.

It is easy to despair.

Yet we have hope and reasons to be hopeful. Everyday in the communities, organisations and people I work with, I see complex problems matched by dedicated people. What gives me hope is watching these dedicated people take the most challenging step in their work—admitting *they* need to learn and change.

My hope is that this book can improve your practice as a leader and be a challenging yet inspiring road to what I think leadership is really about—love.

But more about that later.

Part 1
Understanding the system — the context of change

1
Leadership fantasies

Dreams that do come true can be as unsettling as those that don't.
Brett Butler

THE CALL OF THE FANTASY

Leadership is about making positive change to the world we live in—being useful. This is a noble ambition. We hope things can be better and we think we can play a role in making that progress. If only it were that simple—the reality of implementation makes for grim reading:

- approximately 70% of all change initiatives fail with a heavy human and economic toll;[1]
- less than half of mergers and acquisitions ever reach their intended goals;[2]

3

- more than 68% of executives report unintended side effects of their change initiative, creating new problems instead of solving old ones.[3]

These are a sample of the statistics for organisational change. If we look around our communities at the social issues we face, the statistics are similarly unimpressive. Think about public education, child welfare, climate change, transport in our cities and family violence. The failure to make substantive change in these areas is not for want of trying, or the lack of dedicated, competent people working to make things better.

It turns out most of us have been poorly prepared. Most of what we are taught about making change has consisted of 'foolproof' toolkits, processes and techniques. These can be useful aids. But they can also blind us to some of the deeper dynamics and complexities of what is taking place when we try to make change. As one of my teachers used to say, 'A tool box is supposed to be in our hand and by our side—not in front of our faces.'

Seeing what is really going on can be a challenge. We are often so immersed in the situation that we get lost in it. Yet if we want to be useful, we need to be able to see the bigger, more fundamental process that is taking place between us as human beings when change occurs or is attempted.

Unfortunately, most attempts at change usually start with a *collusion*—a collusion in a fantasy about leadership. We fantasise that our problems will be solved by a mythical saviour or that we will be that saviour ourselves, sweeping away people's problems to great applause and thanks.

Sadly, that never happens. It can be quite surprising that people are uncooperative or ungrateful. Don't they see the problem? Don't they understand I am here to help? Didn't you tell me to fix this?

This fantasy plays out every day. We often hear that 'what we need is some leadership here!' That our leaders need to 'be strong' or 'take control'. Are we asking for leadership or for something else entirely? A saviour? A fall-guy? A servant? A magician? These unrealistic expectations and the confusion about leadership belie this deeper fantasy. In an episode of the Australian current affairs show *Q & A* a climate change panellist summed up this fantasy:

> For me, leadership is making those hard decisions. I want someone to step up and take the lead on climate change in this country, because that's not happening. I want someone to step up and take the lead on indigenous issues in this country, because that's not happening. I want someone to really step up and fight for women's equality in this country, because that's not happening and I want that to happen, and I'm tired of politicians playing around and trying to win, like, sound bites on TV instead of actually doing what they were elected to do, which is fight for our rights—fight for the rights of the generation that's sitting here . . . So that's what I'd like to see in leaders. (*Q & A*, August 6, 2009)

Let's look at what is being expressed here. Firstly, it is an understandable frustration with the way things are. Secondly, it is the hope for someone else to come in and save us all. This is where the fantasy starts. We want someone to do all the hard work. The words are no accident as they are a part of the fantasy for someone to: 'make hard decisions', 'step up', '*really* step up' and 'fight for our rights'.

And, most importantly, 'that's what I would like to *see*'. 'See' is interesting because it is about watching passively. It is no accident that the words 'work with', 'co-operate', 'help' or other more active and participatory words have not been used here. They often aren't when we are talking about leadership. We want a saviour, or perhaps more accurately a gladiator, who will come in and do all the work with as little effort from us as possible.

This is a perfectly reasonable wish. It is always much easier if someone else is willing to do the hard work, put themselves at risk and fight. When I work with groups and begin to talk about leadership, inevitably the names Martin Luther King, Aung San Suu Kyi, John F. Kennedy, Mahatma Gandhi, Jesus and Nelson Mandela come up. These are people who have 'stepped up' and fought. And ended up dead or in gaol for a long time. It's no surprise we would prefer to see than to do.

RESPONDING TO THE CALL

It's easy to get caught up in the fray when we try to lead change and not see the pull of the fantasy. When we as a society, organisation or family have a demand to make things better, someone will supply (at the right price); that's the law of supply and demand playing out. The stage is set and the role of saviour is waiting to be played in the fantasy of 'our problems will be solved and I just need to sit here and watch'.

Enter, stage right, 'the leader': the person with the vision; the person who has all the knowledge; the person with the power (at least at first); the person with the passion; the person with compassion. The demand is there and very seductive. Human systems crave direction, protection and order.[4] We want someone to fix things up, make things better and make us feel better.

It's also a seduction on the supply side of the equation when we offer or are invited to lead. It feels good to be wanted, to have the answers, to be able to see how things 'really are' and to solve people's problems. We all have egos to feed. We are, after all, human beings who want to feel competent and loved. These are basic needs and we have found roles in which we can respond competently to the demand of the fantasy.

We all find our own tested roles, usually without being aware of it. I have worked with many change leaders who are seduced by the 'gorilla role'. This is the person who comes in, beats their figurative chest, bangs heads together and sorts things out: a classic hero role. In my experience, this role is unsurprisingly popular with men, who carry hero ideals much more strongly than women. There are many other roles as well: the teacher, the expert, the helper, the rescuer, the facilitator, the parent. These roles can be very seductive because they connect with something deep within us that gives us comfort and makes us feel competent and needed.

All of this can sound quite sinister or shallow. Seduction and collusion are provocative words. They can indicate a level of malevolent motivations.

It is almost always *not* like that.

We don't wake up in the morning thinking how we can set people up to fail or set ourselves up to fail. It's not that sinister—people are just consciously or unconsciously doing the most convenient thing of handing over responsibility to someone else more willing or able. They may not feel competent enough to do it themselves, lack the energy, not have time or not understand the difficulty of the work involved. They may have been burnt on the last attempt. They may be confused.

From the change agent's view it is not shallow of us to fall into the trap. We genuinely want to make a difference and everyone is calling our name. Why wouldn't we step in? Becoming a victim of this fantasy happens very easily. In this case to me:

It was 2004 and I had just been offered a new position as General Manager of a new division for an international consulting and recruitment firm. 'New' may not be a completely accurate description. As I soon found out, there had been a number of attempts to get this initiative off the ground with no luck so far.

In the recruitment process I heard many good explanations for why this initiative had not worked before and many good reasons for why it would work if I were leading it: my predecessors (two in two years) did not have the right skills and/or attitude; the position had not been given enough autonomy; the position had been given too much autonomy; the rest of the organisation just didn't get it; and there was insufficient executive support. All this may sound familiar to those of you who have been seduced into rescue projects before.

I thought I knew the warning signs of a set-up so I set out to assure myself that I would indeed have the power and support to lead this initiative. I received many assurances. So I gladly, and with some pride, took up the saviour role and entered the fray ready to help.

What I didn't understand was that my investigation and due diligence was actually looking for reassurances that would lead to my own (and the system's) failure to tackle the more complex problem it was facing. I confirmed that the organisation wanted someone to rescue it—not do the hard work it needed to do. All I really did was make sure the demand side of the fantasy was strong.

WHAT'S WRONG WITH THIS PICTURE?

In this case, like in many others, where a system has to do something new and difficult, something that may mean we all need to get uncomfortable for a while, the ground is ripe for leadership fantasies because the work is hard. This is the trap we can fall into if we don't look more deeply at the easy way out the system is trying to find.

I have met many change agents who hear the risks and still want to plough on. We can either get caught so deeply in the trap of supplying against the demand or get some kick out of being the saviour who is willing to pay this price and do what needs to be done to fulfil the fantasy that we can end up being martyrs for our cause. And martyrdom can be very seductive. So what's wrong with that? We all have individual agency and can make decisions about how we utilise ourselves as a resource. This isn't really a problem, is it?

It all depends on the kind of change we are talking about. Ronald Heifetz makes the distinction between two different types of challenges or change: technical and adaptive.[5] These two types of challenges require very different responses from the system and hence different 'work' by those leading change. Technical challenges require the system to do what it already knows to do. Adaptive challenges require that the system learns—adapts. This is where the fantasy and fantasy leaders become problematic.

TECHNICAL WORK, CHALLENGES AND RESPONSES

The vast majority of work happening in any human system is technical work: running IT systems, responding to customer enquiries, dealing with clients, running a transport system, delivering government services. This is the routine work that happens every day and that makes our societies and economies function. This applies to families as much as it does to a multi-national organisation. Our hierarchies and skills have been shaped into creating a way for this technical work to be delivered routinely and reliably. The more a system does technical work, the more the efficacy of the system is reinforced. And, inevitably, the more it stays the same.

Technical challenges can be tackled from the system's existing repertoire of skills and processes. They are relatively easy to diagnose and the solutions are known or can be found. In any human system technical work is what we see happening every day. At an individual level we are immersed in it and our survival is predicated on mastering this work.

This makes it very habitual—particularly given this is the work we are trained and rewarded to do.

But tackling solely technical challenges is not what this book is concerned with; they aren't the challenges that keep you up at nights. These are not the problems where experienced, competent and well intentioned people fail. If you couldn't handle technical challenges you probably would not have got to where you are now.

If we are talking about technical challenges where we fully understand the problem and can find a solution relatively easily, then, yes, we should just go ahead, use the power, hierarchies and knowledge at our disposal and implement the solution or empower others to do so. This is not where the fantasy plays out, but it is where some of the fantasy originates.

ADAPTIVE WORK, CHALLENGES AND RESPONSES

Any human system goes through phases when it is faced with internal or external challenges that require it to change to face these new realities—rather than just look to the leader to fix things. This can happen in many different domains:

- A teenager's shift from childhood to adulthood requires adapting to internal body changes and external changes in our relationships with parents, peers and broader society. We can't rely on our old responses to deal with these shifts—we need to find new responses. For example, we need to start solving some of our own problems rather than turning to our parents as we are accustomed to do.

This is what allows our individual system to adapt. Similarly, our families will find that many of its old responses will not work any more. The family system also needs to adapt and deal with a new reality.

- In organisational life we also face internal and external challenges that require the system to adapt. Internal challenges can include workforce composition and mobility and generational change. External challenges can include changing customer/client demographics, technology shifts, altering societal values and the demand for more transparency and accountability. These shifts require the larger system to adapt and learn. The hero CEO cannot fix these problems alone.

- In society, changes in our environment, migration and ageing populations are just some of the deeper shifts taking place. Once again, the system has to learn to adapt to these new realities if it is to make progress. Hoping our politicians can do this for us is not only unrealistic, it is not where the adaptive work sits.

Every organisation and human system faces some adaptive challenge—usually several. They may be undiscussable or discussed and misunderstood. They can usually be identified as those issues that don't seem to go away. We know from looking at ourselves as an individual system how difficult it can be for us to adapt. Not surprisingly, when we are faced with these more difficult, adaptive challenges, that go beyond our existing repertoire of responses, systems do what they do best: implement technical responses. For example, in organisational life the most common technical responses to adaptive challenges are restructures. Recurring patterns of restructure in an organisation are, in my experience, a technical response to try to address the more adaptive challenges of falling market share, poor customer/client satisfaction, low employee engagement and high staff turnover. Unfortunately, if there was an easy answer that could have just been implemented by the fantasy figure, it would already have happened. Don't kid yourself. Why else do our organisations continuously restructure, for example, while the deeper challenges remain?

As we progress in our careers we find ourselves working with (or pushed into) more adaptive challenges. We are in effect being given responsibility for facilitating learning in a system—even if the challenge and the commensurate adaptation required are not fully understood (as is usually the case) or there is a hope that it can be tackled quite easily. Unfortunately, with adaptive challenges we don't necessarily understand the problem, let alone the solution, when we first encounter it. We usually try to apply existing technologies and approaches (maybe successfully at first), but ultimately we are usually unsuccessful. This is because adaptive problems entail uncertainty and longer time horizons and they challenge the deeper values of the system. In many ways adaptive challenges are very similar to what are called complex problems. Adam Kahane describes a complex problem as:

- *Dynamic*—cause and effect are far apart in space and/ or time. Examples include climate change, black/white relations, public health problems, organisational culture.

- *Generative*—the future of the system is unpredictable and unfamiliar. Examples include company mergers, transition to national independence and democracy (such as in East Timor), and becoming a new parent.
- *Social*—the people who are part of the problem/system have different values, assumptions, objectives, needs and rationales. Examples include migration and settlement issues, the 'glass-ceilings' for women in organisations, tensions between community and corporate expectations.[6]

Yet just calling these problems 'complex', I found, suggests that if we only think about them long enough we can find the solution. It allows us to forget the adaptation: we act like the whole system can implement the one great solution given to us by the fantasy leader and not go through the uncomfortable process of adapting. Adaptive problems are complex **and** they need the whole system to work together to make progress.

This brings us back to the fantasies of leadership. As human beings we do not like dealing with messy, unclear and provocative problems. So the first real concern in trying to fulfil the fantasy is what happens to the change agent. Usually, they become the problem instead because they can't fulfil the expectation of providing an easy way out of the complicated problem.

Nicole works for a global NGO providing services for newly arrived refugees. She is competent, committed and respected by both her clients and her team. The issues she is dealing with are not getting any better. The workload is increasing and the external environment (public attitudes and governmental policy) is getting harsher. Her competence and diligence has seen her rise through the organisation. She now has an opportunity to raise some of the adaptive issues that the organisation is facing at higher levels.

Her views, analyses and recommendations are first met with polite interest, then lack of interest and finally hostility (overt and covert). The organisation is resisting the issues she is raising. These problems are not only hard to look at but dealing with them will challenge the whole system. The adaptation required goes to the core of how the organisation sees itself, the work it does and how it measures its impact. Not surprisingly there is resistance and, inevitably, marginalisation of the individual promoting the adaptation. Nicole is rethinking her occupation and future with the organisation. Indeed some of those decisions may now have been taken out of her hands as she is beginning to be seen as a troublemaker. The system had an expectation that Nicole would fix the problem without everyone having to face the tough issues and adapt.

When the fantasy isn't fulfilled, as it usually isn't, the system has to deal with its disappointment and what it considers to be its error in choosing that leader. The demand for a saviour was not filled correctly so it is time to contemplate new saviours and get rid of the old ones. The applause stops and the accusations start. Getting 'taken out' can take many forms. Change agents get silenced, side-lined, side-tracked, overlooked or removed. In my work with a large Australian corporation, I have found the managers are acutely aware of what happens when you start failing people's expectations. They call this a CLM (Career Limiting Move) or, even worse, a CTM (Career Terminating Move).

The problem is that the system may want things to change, but it doesn't want the loss involved in making the change. The loss is why nothing has happened so far, why past attempts have failed and why people are avoiding the issue. We want to make change and make things better—but not really. We want the gain without the pain.

Some of us are willing to take the risk of being taken out and indeed have worked up very good defences against being taken out. We learn to make alliances, play politics, prepare the ground and, if worst comes to worst, have an exit strategy. However, the bigger issue with solving people's problems for them is that they don't *really* get solved. The issue might become tolerable, but not fixed. Or things begin to work, but only when the change agent is there. When we face new challenges and the old solutions won't work, the system needs to learn. This is the core of adaptive work: *adaptation*.

When there is only a surface change and we don't learn, things usually go back to the way they were pretty quickly. Human systems, from large civilisations down to the individual level, are very resilient in maintaining the status quo. After all, the status quo allows the system to survive now. It is what we know—no matter how bad it may seem. This is particularly so when we are talking about more fundamental, adaptive change, not surface-level technical change: change that may go to the core of what a system values, its identity and how it behaves.

A good case in point for surface level change is what happens to lottery winners. There have been numerous studies which have shown that one of the big fantasies many people have—a large windfall of money—doesn't actually give them what they hoped for—happiness. Things go back to how they were pretty quickly, because nothing has been learned about what leads to happiness for that individual. One of the most cited studies in this area was conducted by psychologists Philip Brickman, Dan Coates, and Ronnie Janoff-Bulman in 1978. They looked at happiness levels of lottery winners and compared them to that of accident victims (who had become paraplegics or quadriplegics). Remarkably, after six months lottery winners didn't report themselves appreciably happier than the control group. While members of the paralysed group did report themselves less happy than the control group, the difference was not as dramatic as the researchers had expected.[7] In some cases things got worse for the lottery winners as they couldn't deal with the 'new opportunities' (parties, increased alcohol consumption, smoking and other risk-taking behaviour). Indeed, while higher income levels usually lead to better health, a decade long study in the UK found that for the National Lottery winners this relationship reversed—and not just in terms of physical health. The sudden windfall actually worsened their lives because they hadn't changed as people.

Not only is there a significant danger that things don't really change, but if the system doesn't learn it is easily led in any convenient direction. In 1895, Eugene Debs (1855–1926), a North American union leader and candidate for President of the United States, addressed a crowd of over 100,000 unionists after his release from gaol:

> I am not a labor leader. I don't want you to follow me or anyone else. If you are looking for a Moses to lead you out of the capitalist wilderness, you will stay right where you are. I would not lead you into this Promised Land if I could, because if I could lead you in, someone else would lead you out.

Debs understood that people need to solve their own problems if there is going to be real change on complicated problems. He understood that fantasy figures and solutions will only lead back to where we started. If we start to think about some of the more complicated, stuck problems we face in terms of *what the system needs to learn*, this is the first step in being freed from our role as saviour and pushes the fantasy into the background. It creates a whole host of new possibilities about what we can do as change agents. Or maybe, more aptly put, learning agents.

This can lead to tough questions. When we are trying to exercise leadership are we promoting learning or dependence? Dependence is easier (and more seductive). It must have been seductive for Debs to stand before 100,000 men at the Chicago Armoury who were looking for direction and had put him on a metaphorical pedestal.

History has shown how easy it is for dependence relationships to develop to the detriment of learning relationships. This is fertile ground for charlatans too. The pain is there and we want an easy way out: we are ready to buy. There have been spectacular examples of charlatans who have offered people the easy answers and met the demand.

We all know the horrors of Adolf Hitler, Joseph Stalin and Idi Amin, to name a few, who offered easy responses to the adaptive problems their countries were facing.

Interestingly, over and over in my work I hear these people described as good leaders—just with bad intentions. It is important to be clear here. In no way were these people exercising leadership. Leadership is about helping the system understand and solve its own problems. They were just very skilled at fulfilling a fantasy—in the short term. And when they inevitability departed, the same problems or new, more difficult problems remained.

Fantasies and dreams do not live long in the harsh light of day. Our dreams have less power over us after a few hours of wakefulness. Though it felt good at the time, we are left with the same fundamental problems.

CHALLENGING THE FANTASY

All this talk about getting caught in a fantasy can feel quite debilitating. It can be easy to interpret this as a call to just do nothing—and let people sort things out for themselves. Exposing the fantasy is not about doing nothing. Instead it is about understanding the temptations to fall into familiar and comfortable patterns which don't really fix anything. We have an opportunity to be much more conscious agents of change. Sometimes this means doing nothing, but usually it is about us being creative and mindful. This will be discussed more deeply in the chapter on compassion.

The first thing is to try to understand what is going on. Hopefully this chapter has shown how easily we get seduced to do the hard work for others and the inherent dangers this represents for us and the system. The next chapter will look at how the fantasy can be activated by the authority we have and how that authority is both an opportunity and a constraint.

REFLECTION QUESTIONS

1. Think about the adaptive challenges you face in your work. What happens when you think about them in terms of what the system needs to learn rather than what needs to change?

2. How do you get seduced into doing the work for others? Is there a particular role that is easy for you to slip into that you keep on playing?

3. What would it mean for you to let go of that role? What might you gain? What would you lose?

2
Authority and freedom

Leadership is the authority that grows ...
Australian Prime Minister Julia Gillard

LOOKING TO AUTHORITY

Understanding the impact and function of authority is the basis for exercising more useful leadership. Authority allows us to:

- get people to pay attention or notice the issue;
- keep them in the room—maintain their attention and energy;
- direct resources to support the work required.

The more authority you have the greater the likelihood that you can get people to pay attention.

Authority is so crucial to the functioning of our lives that we are often blind to it. In many ways it is the air we breathe in our workplaces, families, communities and relationships, whether it is used with purpose and responsibility or abused through neglect and selfishness. Our experiences with authority start early. How authority figures treat us colours how we see the role of authority, our relationship to authority figures and how we step into the role ourselves.

Authority is an inevitable currency of leadership. But the more authority you have, the larger the expectation there is for you to solve the problem. In other words, the larger the fantasy. In a way we shouldn't be surprised that human systems look to others with more power to solve their problems, because that is indeed how we are brought up. We are born completely dependent on our first authority figures: our parents. One of the greatest predictors of social and emotional outcomes is a young child's relationship with his or her primary caregiver.[1] How our parents perform their role can mean, at its extreme, the difference between life and death; and in between—a good start in life and a bad one.

Our first authority figures determine almost everything in our lives and impact our emotional, physical, social and intellectual development. From birth, a child's brain is setting down new connections based on its experiences. Every time a child is hugged, spoken to, played with or read to, new connections are made. Given the many hours usually spent with our parents these connections are made based on their behaviour primarily: whether they pick us up when we fall down, wipe away our tears, hug us and make us feel okay—or not. The impact of this first relationship

Good parent = good boss?

Interestingly, what is seen as important in childhood sounds a lot like what is important from a good boss. Brazelton and Greenspan found that young children have seven 'irreducible' needs: ongoing, nurturing relationships; physical protection, safety and regulation; experiences tailored to individual differences; developmentally appropriate experiences; limit setting, structure and expectations; stable communities and cultural continuity; and adults to protect the future.

'We know that if children get what they need during the first three years of life, they will have a good self-image, an ability to care about others, an eagerness to learn and even a better sense of humor,' observed Dr. Brazelton. 'It is during these years that we have an opportunity for prevention.'

is, needless to say, beyond compare. Children whose parents cannot perform the basic functions of authority struggle throughout their lives. They go on to repeat the patterns of behaviour of their parents because they have learned to regulate their emotional responses to individuals and events through their perception of their caregiver's behaviour.[2]

We carry this attachment though our lives and are programmed to look to authority wherever we go. Think of what happens when the CEO enters the room in your organisation. Or watch how your colleagues check the reaction of the boss to a difficult comment or new idea. This phenomenon is not unique to humans. Many animals share strict hierarchies for their own survival and day-to-day functioning.

More than this, authority figures can embody our dreams and hopes. We have seen this many times in history—in good ways and bad. In his first book, *Dreams from My Father*, Barack Obama recounted his experiences as a community organiser in Chicago. He learned the central role the first black mayor of the city, Harold Washington, played in the lives and minds of Chicago's black residents:

> That's how black people talked about Chicago's mayor, with a familiarity and affection normally reserved for a relative. His picture was everywhere ... displayed prominently like some protective totem ... One thing I noticed, though. The woman so concerned with the cruder habits of her neighbours had a picture of Harold in her kitchen right next to the sampler of the Twenty-third Psalm. So did the young man who lived in the crumbling apartment block a few blocks away ... As it had for the men in Smitty's barbershop, the election had given these people a new idea of themselves. Or maybe it was an old idea, born of a simpler time. Harold was something they still held in common: like my idea of organizing, he held out an offer of collective redemption.[3]

I wonder if Obama has reflected on the parallels between himself and Harold since his own election: how willing we are to build authority up to fantastic proportions. There are many opportunities—and dangers.

SOURCES OF AUTHORITY

The most obvious forms of authority we encounter and occupy are the more formal ones. In organisational life these can be management roles; in family life, our parents and grand-parents; at school our teachers, coaches, prefects and class captains; and in government our elected officials and bureaucracy. These formal sources of authority can have a direct and obvious impact on us when they 'pull rank'.

While formal authority might be the most sought after form of authority it is also the most hamstrung: the expectations on formal authority figures are large and multifaceted. In my work with senior leaders they often express surprise at how little power they have to actually get things done the higher they go. While they can make a big noise and garner attention and resources, they often can't control the direction and level of activity. Think of how many new projects, initiatives or policies that have been launched by CEOs, prime ministers and other leaders which have failed in implementation.

Formal sources of authority are determined by context. I have met many senior managers who come home from a day of being in control to being at the 'bottom of the food chain' in the family. One old colleague, who was responsible for hundreds of people every day on a complex project in Thailand, lamented to me that the family dog got more expensive haircuts than him—in his mind a signal of the (low) level of authority he held in the family context.

Other sources of authority are more informal. This can include 'unearned' sources such as gender, race, culture, birth order, physical ability/disability, religion, money and education. Or they can be earned, through life experiences such as confidence, self-efficacy and knowledge.

In reality we are always working with a mix of these two sources of authority: formal and informal. The mistake we often make is underdeveloping or undervaluing the informal and overplaying our formal authority. This is particularly problematic when talking about adaptive challenges. Firstly because the expectations that formal authority are built upon are usually no longer completely relevant as we are shifting from one state of being to another: the rules change, as do the authority relationships. Secondly, in the disequilibrium that adaptive change generates we actually rely more on sources of informal authority like trustworthiness, psychological temperament, humanity and compassion. Formal structure is less important in the chaos of change.

It can be easy to forget about the important function both formal and informal authority plays when we are thinking about adaptive problems, particularly when some of the authority figures can be part of the problem. But there are many situations where it is important that the tried and tested roles are performed as per expectations: making the status quo work or restoring it when things go wrong. That's called *technical* work.

FILLING EXPECTATIONS—TECHNICAL WORK

From the microcosm of the family to nation states, members of human systems can live or die on the ability of authority to perform its basic functions of providing direction, protection and order.[4] A family's inability to feed its children, keep them safe from harm and provide healthy direction is a microcosm of what happens when a government can't do the same with its citizenry. When a government is corrupt, inept and abusive of its people it ends badly; unfortunately mostly for those whom the government was meant to serve. Burma, North Korea and Zimbabwe are just a few of the better known examples of the failure of authority to fulfil its role. It's very difficult to tackle adaptive problems when we don't have food to eat and aren't safe in our homes or on our streets.

At an organisational level, we see what happens when authority fails to do the necessary technical work and provide clear direction, protection and order. The failure of authority in the now bankrupt Texan energy company Enron is a case writ large. Before becoming bankrupt in 2001, Enron employed over 20,000 people worldwide and was one of the world's leading electricity, gas, pulp and paper, and communications companies. It had reported revenues in excess of $100 billion in 2000.[5] *Fortune Magazine* named Enron 'America's Most Innovative Company' for six consecutive years.

At the end of 2001 it was revealed that Enron's reported financial condition was sustained substantially by institutionalised, systematic, and 'creatively planned' accounting fraud. When the 'Enron scandal' erupted in 2001, it revealed an organisation that was prolifically corrupt.

Yet, Enron did many things right. They broke new ground in different sectors, rewarded innovation, attracted and retained outstanding talent and shifted whole industries. They led wide-ranging adaptation in the sectors they entered.

But those in positions of authority failed to fulfil their basic functions of direction, protection and order.

Direction was lost—the culture became one of just making deals at any cost in almost any industry. While beginning as an energy trading company, the rhetoric morphed in the 1990s to being a 'logistics company'. No one externally really understood what that meant. Internally it meant making deals anywhere and everywhere. As one executive recalls, 'when they found a deal, they did a deal. It was buckshot all over the globe.' Many deals cost a lot more to make than they returned because no one monitored expenses, the costs of making the deal, or what happened to the deal after traders had earned their bonuses and moved onto the next deal.

Protection was missing—Enron President Jeff Skilling recognised the need to manage risk (at least to keep analysts and reporters happy). He set up the Risk Assessment and Control (RAC) department. RAC soon came to be seen as a 'speedbump'. A former Enron managing director describes his relationship with them: 'I treated them like dogs, and they couldn't do anything about me.' So while the processes were there, the group was never protected by people like Skilling and was soon overrun. Protection was also missing for the whistle blowers. Those who started to raise questions about accounting practices, 'cooked' deals or insider trading were shunted, fired or punished in their performance review. The inability to protect those who were concerned with the health of the system eventually led to the collapse of the whole system.

Order fell apart—as the Vice President of Administration until 1998, Mary Wyatt, noted, people just did what they wanted. Expenses were uncontrolled, roles were undefined and structure changed regularly. As businesses folded and opened monthly, employees simply moved to where they thought the action was. So no one really took responsibility, had accountability or learnt a role fully. By 1998, the internal move team were carrying out office moves every night. Enron spent more than $6 million a year just on moving offices and cubicles around.

Ultimately the failure of authority to do the necessary technical work inhibited the adaptive work and brought the company down. In 2001, Enron filed for bankruptcy.

This technical work, and the central role of authority in making it happen, is heightened in times of crisis. This is why war or natural disasters can significantly boost the approval ratings of those in power if they are handled correctly, or be brutally punished if they do not. This usually means making the system do what it is was built to do; that is, mobilising the technical work that allays the fear and insecurities we feel in times of crisis.

We can see how two different crises rewarded and punished the same authority figure, former United States President George W. Bush. Following the terrorist attacks of September 11, 2001 Bush's clarity, determination and mobilising of action (for now let's leave aside whether it was the right action) dramatically advanced his standing in the eyes of the American people. It saved what was on the way to becoming a one-term presidency. The handling of Hurricane Katrina, on the other hand, had the opposite effect. His inability to read the magnitude of the crisis, understand people's fear and loss, and the slow responses of emergency assistance cost Bush dearly.

In Australia, the response of the Federal government to the Bali terrorist bombings in 2002 in which 202 people died (88 from Australia) and hundreds suffered horrific burns and injuries demonstrates how predictable authority needs to be in times of crisis. The Federal Police, emergency medical crews, and evacuation forces were mobilised within 24 hours. Two days later the Prime Minister addressed the parliament and assured Australians that justice would be meted out, that terrorism would continue to be fought and that freedom and security would not be compromised. He also reminded Australians that the response needed to be measured and that Australia was not at war with Islam. Within weeks the Australian Security and Intelligence Office (ASIO) had raided houses in Sydney and Perth of the suspected masterminds of the bombing, Jemaah Islamiah (JI): joint Australian and Indonesian Forces had made arrests in Indonesia and the Australian Attorney General outlawed JI. In addition, the government supported and involved itself in much of the necessary recovery and grieving processes.

The wisdom of some of what was done in this period has been heavily scrutinised. Indeed, there are many adaptive questions that remain following the technical work: are Australians really any safer in Bali or anywhere else due to the government's actions? Does Australia understand why it has inflamed the hatred of people in other countries? These remain open questions. But the government understood and fulfilled its heightened responsibility for providing direction, protection and order at a time when people needed it most. Authority restored equilibrium: it did its job.

It is easy to start to see these patterns and become cynical about the role of authority. This is, however, an unavoidable part of authority's role. We don't judge poorly parents who pick up a child in distress.

ENCOUNTERING PERSONAL AUTHORITY STORIES

Each individual experiences authority differently. Many organisational psychologists contend that how this relationship with authority plays out is linked directly to our early childhood relations with our mothers and fathers and that *we*, in the role of subordinate, are dictating the terms.

If we think of ourselves in this subordinate role, the idea that we choose, create and modify the authority relationships we are in with our bosses (rather than the other way round) is challenging and confronting. Even more so, that we may re-create them again and again (even the bad ones). I have worked with many people who find themselves (exasperatingly) working for the same kind of boss again and again. Or find that their bosses resemble a parent, spouse or ex-spouse.

Yet what might seem dysfunctional in an authority relationship can actually be meeting the needs of the parties involved, quite unconsciously. In many one-on-ones with executives who complain about overly demanding, unreasonable or abusive bosses, these executives are often surprised to see or unwilling to believe how much power they have to change the course of the relationship. This can be difficult to accept because it implies we might actually be colluding in the status quo.

The more complex view put forward here is that we don't simply comply because we think that authority has a right to compel us: we comply to fulfil our fantasies, to appease internalised authority figures, and to cope with emotional conflicts.[6] We legitimise authority because of what *we* seek.

This challenges the conventional wisdom about our relationship with authority. Namely, that we have little agency in dealing with authority and that the model is transactional and static. Moreover that the power differences are irreconcilable.[7]

It may be more useful to look at the relationship as a 'process' between two individuals with a variety of needs and histories, rather than a transaction between a small powerless cog and a big powerful machine. It is not as simple as a passive victim working with an all–powerful structure. If we are able to move away from this simplistic construction of the relationship, we can create more useful options. When we can't, we are stuck with the usual options of compliance or rebellion: the first ones that come to hand—the teenage years playing out again.

Of course there will be authority relationships that are tyrannical, deceptive and deeply abusive: relationships we can't imagine we would actually seek out. The purpose here is not to legitimise this abuse. Rather it is to stop us automatically assuming that authority is transactional and one-way and hence cannot be challenged. Moreover, it may actually be 'followers' who are dictating the terms.

In his work *Meeting God*, Yiannis Gabriel observes that we yearn to identify and idealise our leaders: we project onto

What else have you got?

Many years ago I taught an undergraduate class at a university in Sydney. I enforced what was seen as an unreasonable university rule: that students turn up on time for a class and that being more than 15 minutes late was considered an absence. More than three absences meant failing the course. In the second half of semester, as some students were approaching a precarious position and looked like failing, I asked the class how it was feeling about the rule. There were many emotions: anger (at me), frustration, confusion, relief (that time was no longer wasted in waiting for latecomers to begin the class) and some *schadenfreude* from those who were finally seeing some consequences for the serial latecomers who always disturbed the class. I then asked those who were unhappy with the rule what they were going to do about it. The disgruntled split evenly into those who felt they couldn't do anything about it and were going to bitterly comply and those who were taking it up with head of school (in fact a posse had already been to the head of school's office to complain about me). I then asked them, 'What other options do you have?' After some initial confusion the group realised that no one had actually asked me why the rule was being enforced. Nor did anyone seek to negotiate with me. Compliance or rebellion are almost always our first options. What else have we got?

them our own story of what an authority figure is supposed to do based on our needs. He identifies four dominant narratives:

1. The leader as omnipotent—unafraid and capable of anything.
2. The leader as carer—providing protection and support.
3. The leader as accessible—who can be seen, heard and engaged with.
4. The leader as legitimate—possessing a legitimate claim to the position they hold.[8]

The difficulties in holding authority is that not only do people have different dominant narratives on authority, but also that each narrative is subjective. What I might interpret as a 'legitimate claim to authority', for example, may be different to you. And they are not easily shifted as they are largely based on historical relations (primarily our relationships with our mothers and fathers). In addition, the need carries an emotional charge because the narrative develops from where these relationships may have, in our eyes, failed us—not from what the authority figure did well.

FAILING EXPECTATIONS

When the stakes are so high and the expectations are so diverse, it is almost inevitable that there will be failure. We have all experienced some kind of failure from authority figures in our lives. At its best we see that authority is human: prone to the same temptations and imperfections. This can be hard enough to reconcile; we may feel angry, lost, disillusioned or disappointed. Realising and admitting that your parents, for example, are not perfect is something that is not easy to get over—even when they have good intentions.

And even the best intentioned, calm and loving parents and bosses 'lose it' at one time or another. I think about myself as a parent and despite my good intentions I occasionally will use too much of my power and feel disappointed in myself afterwards. When I confide in other parents I hear, both reassuringly and worryingly, that this happens to the best of us when we are in positions of authority.

Of course not everyone has good intentions. We have all had managers who have made us feel small, looked us over, sidelined or bullied us. Yet the impact of 'losing it' as an authority figure is the same: others will feel worthless, incompetent and fearful.

To complicate things further, authority is always serving many different interests. Not everyone can be pleased all the time. In fact, the higher up you get the more likely it is that you will fail people's expectations, particularly if we are making adaptive change. American President Obama and former Australian Prime Minister Rudd are good examples of this inevitable failure. Coming into office a year apart, both with high expectations and a great deal of hope, it didn't take long before the shine wore off. In Australia, progressives soon shifted their attention to Obama's election after their grand hopes for Rudd were not realised. The same happened to Obama, whose approval ratings dramatically slumped as he waded into the reality of the adaptive issues the USA faced. The stronger the fantasy about the person of authority, the greater the eventual disappointment when the fantasy isn't fulfilled.

In modern life, some theorists have argued that the challenges for authority figures are even more acute due to the 'predominant culture of narcissism'.[9] The strong narcissistic streak in our society simultaneously demands 'strong leaders' and is unwilling to accept a leader's legitimacy for any extended period. The authority figure represents a threat to our ego due to its power. So our relationship to parents and bosses is ambivalent from the start because it is tied simultaneously to a desire to identify with them *and* a desire to replace them. In Freud's words, 'Identification ... can turn into an expression of tenderness as easily as into a wish for someone's removal'.[10]

This turns into unrealistic super-hero requirements for the authority figure that are constantly tested. It is no surprise that we can hold two seemingly contradictory ideas in our mind at the same time: that our politicians are corrupt and untrustworthy, and that they need to take responsibility for and fix all our problems.

THE CHALLENGE OF AUTHORITY (AND LEADERSHIP)

If we comprehend that authority, with all its constraints, is a necessary requirement in exercising leadership, then this creates some new challenges for authority figures.

The first challenge is *understanding* that breaking from the status quo is the work of leadership. Given that the role of authority is largely about maintaining or reinstating the status quo, exercising leadership will undoubtedly threaten our own authority power. This is a fine line to walk. Fail too many expectations and we can lose our authority. Fail too few expectations and we are not exercising leadership. If we think of failure (of expectations) as a withdrawal on our bank account, then as an authority we need to keep a constant eye on the balance so we don't become overdrawn. This is more art than science. It requires a high level of awareness of what is going on around you. How much can I push (fail expectations) here? Do I have enough authority here to push? How can I build it up? Authority and expectations are fluid things—we can't make assumptions about what we have or don't have, what we can and can't do.

An experienced and senior operating theatre nurse once described to me what his work is like. 'When we are in the theatre we all have a hyper-level of awareness. Any move we make with our bodies needs to be thought through before we make it as there are so many instruments, machines and people around us. We can't be thoughtless.' It sounds exhausting—thankfully we are not doing this 24/7. But it is a good analogy. In authority we need to constantly re-evaluate our surroundings and work out 'what do I do right now?', 'what will happen when I do?' The analogy also works because authority power is very constrained. Nothing happens without it, but it is also a bit like a strait jacket. The more we have, the more expectations need to be filled.

The second challenge is *owning* our authority. Abuse and neglect of people and systems comes mostly from not realising or disavowing the power we have in roles of authority—formal or informal. This is understandable; authority and power are provocative ideas in their own right. We have a sensitivity about being seen to be 'power hungry' or on some kind of 'power trip'. This is not what this means. It means actually recognising the power you have and taking responsibility for it and what it can do. The most effective CEOs I have met and worked with understand this. In their presence you have a full appreciation of their authority and it doesn't make you feel small. In a way it's a kind of effortless grace.

This is a big challenge for people in mid-career. As we build our careers we don't have enough authority to do what we want. We understandably want more power, so we can do more. Or people recognise our skills and give us more. We also learn to be humble. You may have been punished for going beyond your authority in the past or noticed how coy people are when talking about power and authority—let alone admitting that we are looking for it. As we advance, we reach a level where we have authority—and most people can see it apart from us. So it is either underutilised or we throw around our weight ungracefully because we might still be clamouring for more, not realising how much we already have. Paradoxically, executives who have been accused of being bullies or heavy-handed usually back off and become much more measured and appropriate when they are given an insight into how much power they have.

The aim is not to perpetuate the abuse nor is it to create dependency. The first step is to own what we have. We can't say we are going to use our authority responsibly if we are not willing to see and admit to it in its entirety.

The final challenge is *accepting* that we can't be perfect or please everyone. The role of authority is actually bigger than any one of us as individuals. It represents a role of providing direction, protection and maintaining order. It also triggers a personal fantasy in those we are leading that these functions will be delivered in a way that suits everyone.

When we think of the 'great leaders' we all know—Martin Luther King, Gandhi, Mandela, Aung San Suu Kyi—we remember them in a way that suits us. We concentrate on their greatness, their insight, their wisdom and their eloquence. In other words, we focus on the fantasy. We don't remember how they gave the work back to people who may not have wanted it. Or how they also divided people. We don't remember what they didn't do, where they failed and how they were human.

AUTHORITY AND FREEDOM

As teenagers we go through one of the most significant periods of adaptation in our lives. Notwithstanding the physical changes happening to us, the break from our parents—the first authority figures—to establish new relationships with the world is the most difficult. For many of us that process never really finishes. Yet the same people we rebel so strongly against are those that we fall back on when things are not as easy as we thought they would be. What happens at these moments is crucial for our own adaptation process: how does authority bring us freedom to make progress?

In 2009, the Australian government apologised to the 'Forgotten Australians'—the more than 500000 child migrants who grew up in institutions, orphanages and foster care. These British migrants were part of a scheme that ran between the 1920s and 1960s and saw (mostly poor) children sent to help populate Britain's former colonies. Their parents back in Britain thought their children would be getting a better life, if they were aware of their children's whereabouts at all. Unfortunately the vast majority experienced nothing of the sort. Many were physically and sexually abused, or made to work as farm labourers in mostly appalling conditions. Survivors to this day still suffer the effects of this abuse.

Five hundred thousand in a country of 20 million people. Add to this those children who suffer abuse and neglect in their families today. And all of us who in one way or another have suffered under an authority figure who abused their power. Our workplaces and communities are filled with narratives about authority—most of them bad. This is the challenge of exercising leadership and using our authority. We have an opportunity to do something different. Every moment we use our power to empower rather than disempower, we rewrite the narrative. We free people.

As I talked about the dilemma of authority to a friend one day, an image came to me. The image was of each of us walking backwards with outstretched arms. One way to think of leadership is of walking slowly backwards with your arms outstretched: creating more and more space for people to solve their own problems, but with protection and purpose provided by you. This is difficult work and there will be push-back for not doing what is usually done: charging forward with you at the front. Turning your back on the goal also represents some of the 'letting go' required. This can be counterintuitive as we have been rewarded and promoted for our ability to have all the answers and be in control.

I wonder if this image can help us to understand the real opportunity of authority: giving people freedom.

REFLECTION QUESTIONS

1. As a subordinate, how would you describe yourself? What 'process' do you engage in with the authority figures in your life?
2. What power do you have that you are willing to own? What power do other people think you have that you are not willing to own?
3. What feelings does the idea of failing people's leadership expectations generate in you?
4. Can you see yourself walking backwards with outstretched arms? What does it feel like?

process do you engage in with the authority figures in

3

Adaptation: the work of leadership

Dubium sapientiae initium.
(Doubt is the origin of wisdom.)
René Descartes

RESISTING CHANGE

Tanya is a forty-something senior executive in an Australian
financial services organisation. She is successful and well-
respected in her organisation. She is competitive (a former
tri-athlete) and is used to success. In the last year she has
started to learn about what it may mean to lead—and not
just fulfil people's expectations:

> I am finding again and again that I am going to meet-
> ings and can see that we are avoiding the real issues.

I didn't realise how much we did that until now and how complicit I was in that. I am not really sure what to do but to ask questions about what is going on. And every time I do, I feel like throwing up. I can see that people are not happy with the questions I am asking, but we are starting to make some progress.

I am trying to get used to feeling like I want to throw up. I don't know what else to do.

Systems made up of people naturally resist change, especially change where there is going to be some kind of loss. Loss can take many forms: fear of the unknown, feelings of incompetence and, of course, that the change will actually make things worse. If we assume what we do will make things better (otherwise there is no reason to begin) and that there isn't much we can do about the unknown, then the one problem we *can* do something about is feeling incompetent. In the modern world one of our biggest fears is feeling incompetent—it doesn't only make us feel stupid, but makes us anxious about losing our job or getting demoted.

Human systems are set up to do things competently—not incompetently. So understandably, most systems have a natural conservatism or resistance to change because the status quo represents that competence. We resist by ignoring the problem, denying there is one, blaming it on someone else or by employing old technology to new problems. We, as leaders of change, also get loaded up with fantasies and this can be exacerbated the greater the authority we have. The system will look to us to fix the problem and maintain the status quo: there is a large investment in being right.

OUT OF THE COMFORT ZONE

The first big mistake in leading change is not understanding that change, particularly adaptive change, is actually a learning process. The work of leadership is to promote and support this learning process. Learning, real learning, in leadership can be hard work. Sometimes we feel like throwing up; we can get inexplicably tired, angry or sad. People want to run away—*we* may want to run away.

Hence the use of the words *adaptive* leadership. For adaptive challenges the system needs to acknowledge the issue, understand it, and start to work on the problem itself. All this involves learning, because if we understood and could fix the problem it would have been done already. It wouldn't be adaptive—it would be technical and therefore an implementation issue for those in positions of authority.

Which brings us to the second big mistake in leading change: imagining we are not part of the problem we are trying to fix. That we are somehow above it, objective and rational. Unfortunately, this is not the case. We are always part of what we are trying to improve. Which means that leading a learning process will inevitably mean we need to learn. We can understand this on an intellectual level; it's not that easy on a practical level.

One of the things I often hear from successful and ambitious people is a wish to 'get out of my comfort zone'. Most of us think that sounds great. We say we love to learn or that we want 'to be pushed'. This is rarely true. What we really mean is that we want to stay in our comfort zone but have a *new* selection of comfortable things to work with: something a bit exotic. We want the Contiki tour of change where we can actually still be right and be competent, where we can learn stuff that adds to what we already know or confirms it.

The people who most often wish to come out of their comfort zone are usually those who are firmly in their comfort zones most of the time: they are doing well, staying on top of stuff, they are respected and trusted. Actually, very little tests them. If anything is difficult it is the volume of work they do which is so large because they can handle it, I dare to say, comfortably.

Kegan and Lahey, in their book *Immunity to Change*,[1] talk about this difficulty as a *competing commitment*. We may have a commitment to learn and change, but if we also have a competing commitment to be right or to deal with change on our own terms then we have a problem.

SKIN IN THE GAME

Our competing commitments to be competent and right are problematic not only for leading change as an individual. It is dangerous in its own right. This is how systems go stale or start to die. At Enron 'the smartest guys in the room' had one fatal flaw: an inability to contemplate that they may be wrong. 'Over time his (CEO, Jeff Skilling's) arrogance hardened, and he became so sure that he was the smartest guy in the room that anyone who disagreed with him was summarily dismissed as just not bright enough to "get it".'[2]

There is a piece of Jeff Skilling in all of us. It's nice to be right and we have been rewarded well for that. That might be okay with technical work, where the solutions are known or can be found relatively easily. With adaptive work it is not that easy—what does *right* mean anyway? The question we are facing might be hard enough to understand let alone finding the answers.

This can become more difficult the more senior we become:

- We are used to having the answers to more and more things.
- We become surrounded, increasingly, by others who are also used to being right or would like to appear so.
- Our authority can become difficult to challenge by those who report to us or who have a lower rank but who might have confronting yet valuable information to give us.

But learning usually means being wrong and not knowing the answers for a while. It means having doubts about what we are doing. We have little training and experience in this—or at least to admitting to others that we don't know. In Chapter 8 we will return to the idea of incompetence and what it means for our ongoing practice.

If we can be humble enough leaders to admit we need to learn, there is a great side benefit. In doing what we might find difficult or would prefer to avoid we are modelling it for others. After all, this is what we will be asking others to do. People will be looking to us to see if we are learning too—do we have any skin in the game? Are we willing to be wrong? Look foolish? Or is it only others (those we may call problematically 'followers') who are supposed to take a risk and look incompetent?

PREPARING FOR THE INNER WORK OF LEADERSHIP

These first three chapters aimed to give a high level overview of the dynamics involved in making lasting, beneficial change. It is by no means exhaustive, but serves to contextualise the core of this book: the development of an individual as a change agent. The following section takes a different tack. It goes into the inner work of leadership and works with the questions that in my experience are most often raised when we start to contemplate our practice as leaders.

Here the path diverges significantly from the unspoken assumptions in the majority of change literature: namely, that we are a blank slate. Unfortunately, most change and leadership literature has colluded with its readers in the idea that we can just assume that we are all the same—we just need to add new processes, qualities and information to whom we are and everything will work. On the contrary, we carry with us our own baggage: the stuff we are proud of; the stuff we would prefer to leave behind; the unique experiences, personality and attitudes that make us us. We cannot act as if this is not how things are: indeed, it may be exactly what the situation requires. In my opinion, the reason most change fails is that it assumes a generic process can be applied to human beings who are anything but generic.

The next section is called *inner work*. This does not mean repair work. This is not a book about fixing or denigrating ourselves. Putting ourselves down is a great way to cover our potential and get us caught in an endless cycle of self-help. It means taking a closer look at some of the inevitable questions and challenges that arise when we start to look at ourselves as part of the mix when making change, rather than fantasising that we are some objective and independent superhuman.

One of the two core skills of any change leader is to be able to stand back from what is going on, or 'get on the balcony'. In the next section we will 'get on the balcony' and take a look at ourselves. When we do this, we encounter new 'work': things that we have to work through, understand and practise if we are to be more useful to others.

How we tackle each of the following pieces of inner work is, of course, different for all of us. I urge you to take time with the following chapters. The issues are not easy ones to work through. Indeed they have been chosen precisely because they are usually stumbling blocks. This is hard work; persevere and take the necessary time. They require contemplation, observation and practice.

In doing this, if you gain nothing else, it will help you build the second core skill of leading: compassion. Looking at ourselves and trying new things gives us some compassion for the process we are putting others through when we lead.

REFLECTION QUESTIONS

1. What do you normally do when you are out of your comfort zone? What are the things that others would see you doing?
2. How do you try to get yourself back in?
3. What might be the risks of getting out of the comfort zone and into your learning zone? Whose expectations might you fail?

Part 2
Understanding ourselves—
the inner work of leadership

4
Power and compassion

But compassion is not so much being kind; it is being creative
to wake a person up.
Chögyam Trungpa

COMPASSION—NOT AN OPTIONAL EXTRA

We can make significant personal progress in our lives
by thinking just about ourselves. There is no denying the
financial and social rewards that come from focusing on
our own personal advancement—especially in the first half
of our lives. We can advance our education, income, career,
relationships and life experiences. In our personal lives
we focus on our pleasure and growth. In our workplaces
we work in our functional area and interact with others
as it serves our functional purpose: working with clients,
customers or colleagues allows us to get *our* work done.

Examining the broader system is not usually on our agenda and we can rarely influence it early in our career anyway.

Then, as we develop, things change. The world asks for more from us—although we may not always hear it or want to hear it. For example, in our:

- workplaces we become increasingly responsible for the health and progress of the wider organisation, not just our immediate function;
- personal lives we may share our lives with a partner or children who require our attention, protection, direction, care and love;
- communities we may engage in new roles in our sporting clubs; professional associations; our children's schools; or cultural, political or interest groups.

This presents us with a challenge: our broader engagement and responsibilities require us to think differently of those around us. This does not mean leaving personal interest behind but rather finding a way to be useful beyond ourselves—as we are called by our organisation, family or community to protect and develop their collective future.

This is more than a philosophical shift, it's also a practical one. Leadership is a social pursuit: we need other people's help to make progress—their effort, motivation, ideas and skills. This applies whether we are talking about staff, colleagues or families. The challenges we face can rarely be tackled alone—particularly as we are increasingly given responsibility to coordinate and direct the work of others on complex, adaptive issues.

We need to learn how to think about our work with and for others in a useful way. We haven't been trained to do that—we have been trained to work alone. If we want resilient and healthy organisations and communities this means making a conscious decision to ensure those we lead can grow rather than just be dependent, grateful or obedient. We need to ask ourselves: Do we want to create followers or leaders?

The work of leadership is building people's capacity to be the leaders of their own lives, communities, organisations and families. This means good leadership is inevitably an act of compassion because we are looking to develop people's ability to understand and solve their own problems.

This is not the common understanding of compassion: we usually think of compassion as being kind. Compassion is much more than being kind. We can easily delegate

But what's in it for me?

There is more to compassion than being beneficial to others: it is also beneficial to us in exercising leadership. In fact, compassion can be good for your health. There have been numerous studies that have shown how even just having positive, loving thoughts about others improves our health. This is good to know given the strains of exercising leadership. A 1995 study by Rein, Atkinson and McCraty looked into the effects of feeling care and compassion (CC) versus anger and frustration (AF) on the production of S-IgA, an important antibody in the upper respiratory tract. This antibody is frequently used as a measure of secretory immunity. Thoughts and feelings of CC significantly increased S-IgA levels. Moreover, the effects were more pronounced when these feelings were internally induced (through the subjects focusing on the feelings of care and compassion towards someone or something) rather than externally triggered through images. This tendency towards increased levels of S-IgA was observed over six hours.

In 2006, Boyatzis, Smith and Blaize looked at the impacts of 'coaching with compassion' as a means of lessening the impacts of 'power stress'. [1] This type of stress is associated with the exercise of power in positions of authority: the feelings of responsibility these roles entail and the exercise of self control. The experience of power stress arouses the sympathetic nervous system (SNS), triggering flight-or-fight responses and, over time, leads to the release of immunosuppressants. So repeated activation of the SNS makes the body susceptible to infection, heart problems and gastrointestinal problems.

Coaching with compassion was defined as 'helping others in their intentional change process' as distinct from the typical intent of coaching—developing a supply of leaders for the organisation. This type of coaching will stimulate internal processes that enable leaders to balance the toxic effects of power stress inherent in their roles as leaders.

kindness—to others who are running charities, to another part of our lives where we can be generous with our families or with financial donations. We can leave it at the door, turn it on when we remember or it suits us, or leave it to others we think more suited or interested.

Compassion is about taking responsibility for the growth and development of other people. This kind of motivation is actually every leader's work—in every industry and profession. Without this motivation we are on our own with the power we have rather than using it to benefit our world and work. Without this motivation we aren't really leading.

RETREATING FROM RESPONSIBILITY: KINDNESS OR FLIGHT

Benefiting our systems and the people in them is important but hard. In my work with leaders who try to develop themselves to meet this challenge, I have seen two main stumbling blocks: focusing on kindness or becoming overwhelmed, which turns to flight.

While it is important to be kind in everyday life, compassion is something more than that. While compassion promotes growth and development, kindness might actually be what is holding the problem in place. Out of kindness we don't tell someone how they are making things worse or not helping. Out of kindness we give people what they want in the short term to the detriment of the long term. Out of kindness we protect people from a difficult truth. Some of us also know that being kind can mean we are taken advantage of. For people running organisations and projects, kindness can hurt the whole system; we have mandates to do our work and what we think of as kindness to one person or group may hurt the whole system.

Not only can we be taken advantage of, we can also end up hurting ourselves or those we hoped to help.

A number of years ago a friend of a friend came to stay for 'just a few days'. We soon found out that she was suffering from anorexia-bulimia. Initially feeling quite sad for her and her story, we heard how she really wanted to make a change. We saw an opportunity to support her and offered for her to stay to sort it out. Somehow this act of kindness ended in resentment, frustration and anger from both sides within just a few weeks. We eventually asked her to move out, which resulted in screams and tears of protest.

I was confused by how this went from what I thought was compassion to anger in such a short time. How did I go from opening up to shutting down so completely? I felt idiotic — and hopeless.

When we are focused on being kind we can become overly concerned with helping rather than being helpful. This inevitably means there is a 'helped' or 'helpless' other: people who need to be helped by us or cared for by us. While we need to care for others we need to be careful it doesn't end up impeding their growth or harming ourselves. Buddhists call this kindness Idiot Compassion. If we look around our society we can see many of these reciprocal (and 'stuck') relationships in place. One welfare organisation recently described this to me: 'We realised that we kept on feeding people and nothing ever changed for them. They had learned the "shape of our spoon".'

Pity is the most obvious symptom of this dynamic as it can easily arise when we take the role of helper. We can develop quite a romantic view of helping that often means we don't really engage with or feel the pain of the helped: we remain quite separate. It might be easier to help poor people on the other side of the world whose pain is far away from us. In that way we don't have to deal with the reality of these people as human beings. Up close human beings are a lot less romantic. It feels safer to have distance—this distance may not be physical; it can also be social and psychological. If we think of the old model of charities we can quickly conjure up images of well-meaning rich people building orphanages.

Kindness is not the only challenge. Taking responsibility for your system and the people in it can be overwhelming, tiring or frightening. We might run instead. So we may not tell a colleague or subordinate that they are not performing because they are fragile, come from a minority group or are difficult to deal with. We create a wide berth filled with cotton wool and ultimately, unwittingly, ensure they can never get out of the spot they are in—we keep them stuck in their place.

Ahmed is a project manager in his mid-30s working on a large construction project. He has 'inherited' a team of senior engineers to work on his part of the project. He soon finds that one of the engineers, an older man in his fifties, is not capable of doing the work he is meant to do. When he seeks advice from his own manager, Ahmed discovers that it was well known that the older engineer had not been performing at a suitable level for many years. He had been palmed off from one project to another for over a decade. Not surprisingly, when Ahmed takes up the problem with the engineer he faces an angry backlash. The engineer claims he has never before been told about poor performance. Ahmed guesses that the engineer probably knew he hasn't been up to the job for a while and people's unwillingness to be honest with him had 'inflamed' the engineer even more than the conversation with Ahmed.

I have seen these situations play out many times in my experience as a manager and consultant. Often they end up in court as the employee in question, quite rightly, contends that they had never been told about their poor performance. Whether it's fear or kindness, ultimately, we block the person's growth: either in their current role or to another job. We also damage the system. Poor performance and lack of consequences impact the motivation of other employees and undermine the authority and trust of those in positions of authority.

Running can take many forms. We can 'flip' from ignoring the problem or being overly kind to being harsh and uncaring. We can become quite aggressive and end up laying our agenda on the other person. Collette Livermore, an Australian woman who served as a nun for Mother Teresa for eleven years, talks about this in her work with the Order. 'The sisters were corrected very harshly, and humiliated verbally and that sort of thing, so that they would become humble . . . we were never meant to ask why or disagree with anything, or give our opinion about things, we were just to do what we were told. Total surrender was what Mother asked of us.'[2]

I have seen this 'spillage' of anger and harshness many times in organisations that dogmatically aim to serve without question, yet at great personal cost. The smiling faces with clients outside are often quite hostile within the organisation.

Nicole, one of Social Leadership Australia's program alumnae, worked for eight years with a major humanitarian organisation involved in helping refugee communities. She tells a similar story of her work. The unquestioning focus on helping became a sort of 'internal Marxism', as she puts it, where staff became harsh and overly demanding with each other. 'When you do this work for a long time, there's an anger. I don't know if you can do this work for so long and not get angry. Maybe, it's not the compassion that makes people tired, it's the anger. How do you manage the anger or does it manage you?' This is not only a concern for those who are seeking to be useful and make progress, but also for the legacy left behind. Who will be inspired to follow such a path?

Our flight from compassion (and hence leadership) can take another shape. We might feel that it is just too hard and people are too difficult so we 'float' above or away from the challenge involved. We might think that whatever we do is to no avail or we don't know what to focus on. This is a typical middle and senior management problem. We know we have to take an interest in others and their development, but we find it too hard and shift the responsibility to the CEO, the human resource department, consultants or executive coaches.

What all these blocks have in common is some kind of expectation of:

- getting it right or 'fixing' the problem;
- how people should react or behave;
- maintaining control.

The experience with my house guest was a great example of this. Just because I was making the effort doesn't mean she was ready or able. Nor did it mean that what I had to offer was useful. What if my efforts were actually making things worse? As such it also reflects an unwillingness to work with how things and people really are—and with how we really are.

Not surprisingly, this can slide into personal distress and fatigue. It is no wonder we instinctively pull back from opening ourselves up too much or exposing ourselves, and instead retreat to safer ground.

Crisis of faith, compassion fatigue or kindness fatigue?

Compassion's slide into personal distress and fatigue is unfortunately all too common. It can lead easily to what I have heard described as 'compassion fatigue'. If you ask a group of people to think of the most compassionate and kind person they know of, Mother Teresa's name will usually surface. Mother Teresa was a Catholic nun who founded the Missionaries of Charity in Calcutta. For 45 years she worked for the poor, sick, orphaned and dying until her death in 1997. When her secret letters to her spiritual guides were released in 2001, many were shocked that the person who is so often held out as the icon of compassion felt such a deep level of emptiness and desolation.

Now Father—since (19)49 or (19)50 this terrible sense of loss—this untold darkness—this loneliness —this continual longing for God—which gives me that pain deep down in my heart. Darkness is such that I really do not see— neither with my mind nor with my reason. The place of God in my soul is blank. There is no God within me . . . God does not want me. Sometimes—I just hear my own heart cry out—'My God' and nothing else comes. The torture and pain I can't explain.

Where I try to raise my thoughts to heaven, there is such convicting emptiness that those very thoughts return like sharp knives and hurt my very soul. Love—the word—it brings nothing.

These excerpts from her letters are not isolated incidents from low points in her life—they are part of decades of inner torment and doubt. It is distressing that someone who devoted her life to helping others should feel this way. This could be called a crisis of faith if it wasn't for the fact that many who seek to 'help' often get so tired and disillusioned. The problems are so large, sad and confronting that our only response is to be kind or run. Both are ways of protecting ourselves. They are exhausting and not helpful.

EQUANIMITY: NO HISTORY, NO DESIRE

When we start to see these as less useful ways of taking on our responsibilities as compassionate leaders, we can begin to get an idea of what an alternative reality might look like. Maybe the reason why 'real' compassion (and, by implication, leadership) is so hard to do and so seldom seen is because it requires us to do something we don't do very often: be in the present. This means coming into the moment without history or desire. Our history includes our past experiences, prejudices and former relationships. Our desire is how *we* want things to be for the people we are working with based on *our* personality and personal preferences. It is also our desire to be selfless, caring and not needing any help for ourselves. All of this stops us being in the moment and seeing what is required based on what is happening in front of us. Our judgements and passions hinder us, as subsequent chapters will discuss.

It might be useful to think of compassion as an activity, like leadership, rather than a state: it is something we *do*. And what we do has an opportunity to be completely in the present, whereas who we are is heavily influenced by our history and our desires. Compassion without history and desire brings equanimity—a more even mind or temperament, more often referred to as balancing our heart with our head. We can make New Year's-style resolutions to do that (which usually fail) or we can find some more practical ways of bringing this equanimity.

Firstly, we can replace *fixing* with *listening*. Nicole told me about this experience with her clients: 'When I am working well, I am listening with openness and really being present for people. I can't tell you the amount of times when I have done bugger all for people. Yet I hear from them much later and they say "you can't believe what you did for me that day". Sometimes I can't even remember that person.'

I would argue that there can be no real compassion without listening—really listening. Regardless of any fixing, there is *the fix that is listening*. The process itself can do more than we really understand.

Many years ago I worked for an outplacement firm. Our job was to help organisations 'transition' people out of the organisation, which is a nice way of saying firing people. We would turn up after people were notified of their termination and begin a coaching relationship. In our first meeting, right after they got the news that they had lost their job, we knew most people couldn't actually hear anything—they couldn't digest any information about their financial packages, future plans or the relationship we were starting with them. All we could do was listen to what they were feeling. While it no doubt helped their now-former employer by giving their ex-employees a place to vent, which wasn't a courtroom, it invariably helped the individual too. Listening was the most compassionate thing that could be done for them. And we saw in most instances we were the only people in their lives who could do that without judgement, expectations or loading them up with 'helpful' quick fixes.

REPLACING 'SHOULDS' WITH TRUST

We can't always know exactly what the right thing is for the people we are working with. It is often easy to see what is not useful. It is much harder to know what the right way is and when people will be ready to change.

We can only do what we can and of course it will not be perfect. We can become wiser, but we need to not be aggressive about it. Many times we just need to let people do what they need to do and let them know we support them and that there are other possibilities. In a way this requires a level of trust—of them and their progress.

Sometimes we have a problem trusting that ultimately people will decide for themselves about when they will change. This can be hard to accept if we see them hurting themselves. This doesn't mean we don't protect them and those around them from real harm, but we can't get caught up in thinking about how people *should* behave. Pretty soon we'd start reacting to maintain boundaries and stop ourselves being exploited. This is perhaps where some of the 'compassion fatigue' comes from as we become exploited or overworked ourselves. In the words of Chögyam Trungpa: 'Openness doesn't mean you have to take everything in at all; you have the right to reject or accept—but when you reject you don't close *yourself*, you reject the situation.'[3]

Our trust needs to be tempered with setting boundaries. After all, we want to be around to fight another day. Compassion is not some endless, bleeding, open heart. This is important: sometimes the best thing to do is to walk away. We do that not because we are scared or exposed but because we cannot benefit the situation. And we remember that there is an opportunity cost to our time. Is what is in front of me the best use of my compassionate time and energy?

Ask yourself: Is this having the greatest impact for the most people for the longest time?

REPLACE CONTROL WITH CREATIVITY

Trust requires us to understand that we are not in control. If we feel that we have to be in control of what is happening and how people are reacting we will harden up and not have the necessary creative intelligence to actually be useful for people. This is the other way that compassion is linked to leadership—it is a creative process.

So how does listening, trust and creativity apply in daily organisational life or when working on complex issues? Firstly, it can be applied in many of the small interactions we have with people, whether it is about managing performance or checking in on the wellbeing of employees or clients. Being compassionate (or useful) means understanding the fix that is in listening (rather than just fixing), creatively helping people when they are stuck, letting go of being in control of how they should do it and trusting people to find their own way there and to use us when they are ready and able.

It is also important in big changes where we can't make things better for people or when the change is an edict, for example, in organisational downsizing. Sometimes we don't have anything to give people but our ears and our presence. We are all that is providing direction, protection, order and care. Sometimes that is all we can do compassionately for the 'casualties' of our organisations, of victims of abuse or neglect or people dealing with their own personal problems.

When we do this we can start to really develop some compassion—and leadership. That requires us to connect with a more exposed part of who we are. We can spend time trying to work with the situation rather than trying to protect ourselves. And slowly we become 'more curious than afraid'.[4]

WHERE TO START: COMPASSION FOR OURSELVES—CREATING FLUIDITY

It sounds trite to say we should be compassionate with ourselves. Surely there are people much more worthy of compassion than me! That might be so, but when we are not compassionate towards ourselves it affects our practice as leaders.

Firstly, it is not being realistic. We are human and susceptible to old age, sickness and death. We hurt, fail and are not treated how we would like. We can't remove ourselves from the reality of what it means to be a human being. We need to stop thinking of some super-hero version of compassion. If we can't be compassionate with ourselves we will ultimately burn out. We need to recognise the need to look after ourselves and not just be thinking of others all the time. For example, I probably shouldn't go and talk to the person who drives me most crazy when I am feeling tired, sad or upset.

This realism about ourselves creates the most important shift we can hope for: role fluidity. That is, fluidity between the role of helper and helped. If we can see that we need help, need to be cared for and are at times helpless, then we are not projecting all of those uncomfortable realities onto other people. If those we are trying to benefit have to own all of the 'helped' role, they will never have a chance of releasing themselves from this to take another role—that of the helper and the carer for their own lives and others. In other words, we never give others the opportunity to transform from followers to leaders.

Secondly, when we see that we are also susceptible to all the same problems that are worthy of compassion, we can use ourselves as a case in point to explore humanity. We can become greater experts on anger, jealousy, self-deprecation, incompetence, sadness and loss. This gives us insight into other people's lives and problems in a real way—not a safe, theoretical way.

SO WHAT IS COMPASSION, REALLY?

Compassion is an *activity*—an activity that recognises the reality of our lives and others' lives. It is built on a motivation to take beneficial steps to improve lives—including our own. I have seen that when we do this with the skill and mindfulness of allowing others to grow and learn it brings us happiness too. Luckily, we all have the ability to bring this motivation to life. We just need to find *creative ways of waking ourselves up.*

Compassion is a kind of love. And we all know from relationships that loving feelings are not enough, as they soon dissipate when circumstances change or our expectations are not met. Compassion requires a good understanding of how things work. Its enemy is judgement.

Wisdom is the next chapter.

REFLECTION QUESTIONS

1. What would change in your work and workplace if you approached some of the more difficult groups or issues you are facing with the question, 'How can I benefit the situation?' Try it before your next tough meeting.

2. What part does anger and fear play in your compassionate motivation? What would it take to be compassionate without anger and fear?

3. How could creativity play a role in compassion for you? What shift would that mean in the role you play? Or how you are seen?

5

Wisdom not judgement

Housing commission hell! It's the infamous Northcott building at Surry Hills. The scene of countless murders and suicides over the years; five deaths in the past 12 months. It's a slum! With criminals, drug addicts, the mentally ill, the elderly and, unfortunately, children. All living together in fear, in hundreds of shoe-box sized apartments . . . Nothing surprises the residents here any more: daily domestics, tenants defecating in the lifts, stolen cars torched and dumped here; used heroin needles dropped in the flower beds. They're life's forgotten people. They need help but they are just not getting it.
Channel 10 News, Sydney, August 2002

This television news report on the Northcott public housing estate in Sydney was typical of the coverage the estate received from the media. Northcott had a number of colourful aliases: 'Death Estate', 'Housing Commission Hell' and 'Suicide Towers'. One of its residents described his life there as living in the *Starship Enterprise* as it was so different to normal life on earth. The estate comprises three high-rise buildings, over 14 storeys high and accommodates over 1000 people. The popularity of these mega-estates spread from Sweden to the US and UK and to parts of Australia in the 1950s.

Fifty years later and the suburb held the unenviable position of the state's number one hotspot for assaults, break and enter, and motor vehicle theft. On the estate, police attended an incident 1.7 times per day. The profile of residents had changed from predominantly lower socio-economic, working class people to a much more complex mix. Sixty per cent of residents were now aged over 60; the estate housed 50 different nationalities; 30 per cent of residents had mental health issues; and drug and alcohol issues were significant.

When Channel 10 ran its story the estate had gone into significant decline. Residents wouldn't leave their flats, drug dealers worked the buildings and any community spirit that was there to start with had significantly eroded. Residents talked of routinely seeing furniture being thrown from balconies. Some of the lighter debris, such as irons and computer peripherals, could be seen hanging from trees like strange exotic fruits. To say that Northcott seemed like a hopeless situation would have been an understatement.

Fast forward four years from the news report and many things had changed at Northcott: the World Health Organization (WHO) had accredited Northcott as a Safe

Community; the Community Centre had been revitalised and is now run by tenants—not the Department of Housing; there have been two shows about the estate in the Sydney Festival (one in a transformed car park on the estate); and a documentary called *900 Neighbours* screened on ABC Television after being a hit at the Sydney Film Festival. Most significant and surprising is the collaboration: between tenants, the police and the arts community.

Somehow this community had shifted from people living in collective fear and decline to a level of functioning no one would have imagined in their wildest dreams.

How did this happen?

LOOKING FOR CERTAINTY

Northcott has been the object of many judgements over the years. Its residents have faced prejudice throughout their lives due to their socioeconomic state, their mental health or cultural background. Northcott was conceived out of a well meaning decision to ensure low income people were no longer subjected to the 'dangers' of the private housing market. Indeed, its own residents passed routine judgements on the plight of the estate. As a resident interviewed for the Channel 10 news report commented, 'I reckon they should bulldoze this place and start again.'

In among all these judgements—well intentioned and otherwise—a small group of people, and one person in particular, were able to put their judgements aside and make change happen *with* people on the estate.

In 2002 a local member of parliament, Clover Moore, successfully lobbied the state government to assign a community worker to Northcott. That worker, Dominic Grenot, soon joined forces with a Crime Prevention Officer, Brett Degenhardt from the police local area command, and with Big hArt, an organisation that ran community-based arts projects.

Dominic soon found that many firm judgements had been made about the residents, about what should be done and about what does and doesn't work. There were some pretty clear ideas on what he should and shouldn't be doing—and how long it would take. He was given three months to 'turn things around' in a problem that had been building over decades. Interestingly, he found much of the certainty came from very little actual knowledge, let alone wisdom. In the briefing for the role with his new boss he soon found that his superior had never actually been to Northcott.

Indeed, when Dominic arrived at Northcott and talked to other Department of Housing staff he found that they rarely, if ever, walked across the road from their offices to the estate. One reason for this was fear for their safety. Community health workers, for example, would only come onto the estate in pairs. The deeper reason was more about psychological safety: that of not having to confront some well formed assumptions and judgements on what was going on.

When we are afraid, we look for certainty—points of stability. Our judgements provide that for us. They give us an easy way to navigate through the inconvenient, confusing, irritating or troubling.

WHAT JUDGEMENTS (DIDN'T HAPPEN) AT NORTHCOTT?

A judgement had already been made about Northcott and its residents when Dominic first walked onto the estate. Indeed it had been made a long time before that. The unwritten agenda was to make sure it didn't get in the news any more. Thankfully, there was a group of people who hadn't made such a conclusive judgement.

But really looking at what is going on can be scary. Interacting with it is a threat to our self-assured lives. Think of all the issues in your organisation or relationships that are labelled as 'no-go zones'. They are no-go because we fear what will happen if we have to leave the safety of our judgements for a while and go into the unpredictable zone of not knowing what will happen. Instead we put them in the 'parking lot' or say they are 'not on the agenda today'.

Dominic realised and was able to see and admit to his fears (if only privately). He recounts his difficulties in those first few months: 'I would walk across the road and just stare at the buildings. It was mesmerising—like looking into a fire.' The immensity of the task was overwhelming and at first paralysing.

As one of the tenants confided to him, 'we have to create a new normal'. But no one could define what this new normal meant, let alone how to get there. Indeed, all the department could define was what they *didn't* want: no more crime, no more suicides and, most of all, no more bad press. It was at this point that Dominic realised that the traditional approach of defining a future state and the steps along the way probably weren't going to work. As he put it, 'I couldn't see the point of trying to create a future that we couldn't conceive from a place we didn't understand.'

Instead, Dominic started *listening* and *working with what was there.* He listened to residents in a way they hadn't been listened to before and committed to meeting every resident on the estate. Armed with a 'survey', he used this as an excuse to talk. He did lots and lots of listening in his first few months and indeed in his whole time there. Unsurprisingly, tenants felt that they had never really been heard. The effect of the listening was firstly one of venting. Some tenants had a lot to get off their chests: anger, fear, sadness and, for many, loneliness. This is not unusual—at the heart of any marginalised group are people who feel they have not been heard but have been judged.

He *partnered* with other organisations, particularly police. This became an important alliance. Brett was able to shift the tenants' view of the police from a threat to protectors of 'the new normal'. This filtered all the way into the Local Area Command where 'good news stories' about Northcott would be broadcast on internal police TV, giving Brett the space he needed to continue the unorthodox approach he was using of working with the community rather than just policing it. Brett also allowed Dominic to play 'good cop' when they worked together, further building tenants' trust in Dominic. This partnering is unique as so often in difficult problems we find groups of people *going it alone*, sometimes with all the trappings of martyrdom. They often come with their own set of judgements of 'no one else understands' and 'if it wasn't for me, no one would care!'

The partners were *creative* in overcoming some of the barriers of trust. By using different methods of storytelling, tenants were able to build confidence again in themselves and in their neighbours. For example, one project, 'Tenant-by-Tenant', involved tenants taking portrait-style photos of each other with the aid of a professional photographer. This built connections and trust between tenants and a strong sense of their own worth. These connections became a critical part in the tenants taking action for themselves. The credo was 'if you know someone's story it is much harder to hurt them'.

Creativity is the real jewel here—and judgement kills creativity. Our judgements block us being creative because if we have already made a judgement then everything is already concluded: there is no more potential in the situation.

Dominic and Brett *created spaces* where tenants could become involved in a way they felt comfortable doing, an approach called 'open crowd'. This became a keystone of the transformation approach at Northcott. This meant that at any event, meeting or social gathering concerning the estate everyone was invited, so there were no in-groups or out-groups among the tenants. Tenants could then engage at their own level of readiness and capacity when and how they saw fit. In effect, this meant that tenants were guiding their own personal change journey. This also meant that change would always start from where people were at, leveraging the skills people already had.

JUDGEMENT HAS HAD ITS DAY

People with good judgement are promoted, given important assignments, paid well and generally well respected. We put our lives in the hands of men and women who we think possess the capability to make good judgements: doctors, nurses, pilots, engineers, politicians and, of course, judges. We commend those who make 'good judgements'.

But I am not so sure of the value judgement serves in leadership. This probably sounds revolutionary—or at least countercultural—as judgement is so highly rewarded. When we face problems that our judgements and many other people's previous judgements have not fixed, these are adaptive problems.

In my work with organisations and communities that want to change and individuals who want to facilitate change, I see that judgement (good or otherwise) is not enough. In fact it is not only insufficient, it promotes the wrong questions and by implication the wrong answers. Indeed, many of the problems a community, an organisation or a relationship faces are held in place and created by judgements. In one broad sweep we can limit all possibilities by the judgements we make about people: our politicians, teenage mothers, refugees who 'jump the queue' and people on the right or left side of politics.

It's easy to understand; it makes things simpler to deal with when we can put someone or something in a box and label it. Then we don't have to think about it any more. It's a big world and there's a lot to do. Elections have been won and lost on playing to our desire to quickly make a judgement so we can move on and stop wondering what to think and do about the issues we face.

This is where it starts to get complicated. You might be thinking, 'hang on, judgement is important in many daily activities'. I agree it is very convenient to have the capability to judge the distance of an approaching car when crossing the road or to have a doctor who can judge whether we need to undergo an operation immediately or just cut down on our dairy foods. But these are judgements about *things*. It's when we start to extend judgement to how we interact as humans and the way in which we address the problems we face as a society that judgement starts to fail.

This is not new thinking. Many of the more evolved and humanist religions and philosophies have been encouraging us to not judge our fellow man for a long time. But this is easier said than done. We are instinctively and unconsciously making judgements every minute. At any one moment we are thinking, talking or acting in a way which reflects these judgements: 'I don't like that!', 'I like that', 'they are not like us', 'that's clever', 'he is offensive', 'she is a team player', 'they are stupid' and so on. We are organic, mobile judgement machines. Listen in on any congregation of people and you will very soon hear a stream of judgements about politics, films, food or acquaintances.

Listening to teenagers talk is even more enlightening. Their interchange is almost exclusively judgemental, as they jockey for social standing and find their way in an adults' world of judgement. In fact generations define themselves with language shortcuts which judge others and things: 'cool', 'wicked', 'sick', etc.

Judgements are even entertaining. Shock-jocks have made a living through their ability to freely and convincingly express judgements on any particular issue. Tabloids sell newspapers through a front page headline which judges something or some other: refugees, terrorists, people of Middle-Eastern appearance, immigrants, dole bludgers and whole geographic communities.

But we can look around us and see how the judgements we, or the people we vote for, make are just not cutting it. I don't see any positive impact in the judgements we make about people, communities or values. Ask yourself what has judgement done for you lately? What relationships has judgement improved? What new insights has it generated? Where have people been able to work together in new ways because of judgements they have made about each other?

WISDOM COMES FROM NEW QUESTIONS (NOT OLD JUDGEMENTS)

Maybe it's time for a new question, a question that puts aside our patterns of judgement and allows us to work with people and communities in a fresh, *non-judgemental* way. We know that just saying 'don't judge' and trying to be 'more open' probably won't do it. But what to do instead?

How about a question that allows us to enter a situation thinking how we can *benefit it*? What if we entered the room with: 'How can I benefit this situation?' If we are focusing on how we can bring benefit to a situation—real benefit, not just a quick fix—there is suddenly a lot more space. Suddenly there are options that open up: rather than people, problems or ideas that are shut down with our judgements.

Imagine entering conflict in our marriages, our work-places or culture with 'How can I benefit this?' What are we freed to do? What wisdom can surface? When I have met with people like Dominic over the years, I am repeatedly struck by their ability to be present and how they decide to be useful from where they are right now. But it can be unnerving as it sounds quite open-ended, empty or goalless.

> I haven't stopped wanting someone, somewhere to return with the right answers, but I know that my hopes are old, based on a different universe. In this new world, you and I make it up as we go along, not because we lack the expertise or planning skills, but because that is the nature of reality. Reality changes shape and meaning because of our activity. And it is constantly new. We are required to be there, as active participants. It can't happen without us and nobody can do it for us.

As Margaret Wheatley[1] points out, this does not mean we leave behind our plans, skills and experiences or indeed the uniqueness of who we are—good and bad. It is more about being present to what is required in the moment and being free to actually exercise leadership rather than being on a judgement auto-pilot. This leaves space for a new kind of wisdom, one that has a firm foundation—curiosity.

CURIOSITY, WISDOM AND TRUST

Let us begin with the idea that the situation can bring the solution. This can be hard to accept, particularly if we have a strong view that we are responsible for providing the solution. We may even have been hired with the express purpose of bringing our expertise and fixing the problems.

The idea that people have their own solutions can be difficult to see or accept sometimes. Perhaps then just 'rent' the idea for a while—it can be 'purchased' later if it works.

We have very few reference points for this kind of idea. Sometimes we have to dig deep in our memories. It might be a particularly good teacher you had, a manager or coach who saw your potential, or a 'wise' friend who asks the rights questions or allows you to talk. Sometimes what they are doing is only clear when you think of what is absent— judgements of you and others involved in your issue, fixing your problem, bringing their own problems/issues and hang-ups into the mix. I suspect their wisdom comes from their curiosity in us. The curiosity allows the situation to generate its own wisdom. Once again it is important to remember here that we are talking about adaptive issues—one where the system needs to learn something to move forward.

This requires trust. And trust is difficult. In much of my work with organisations that are stuck in a problem this word arises. People don't trust their leaders, they don't trust their colleagues, they don't trust their staff, and some don't trust their customers or clients. In my work with an organisation working with at-risk and disadvantaged young people, I asked whether young people could be involved in creating a piece of work we were doing. I was told: 'If young people knew what they wanted, do you think they would be coming to us?'

Often this lack of trust has good reason. We have had experiences that make us fearful and wary, experiences where we were cheated, used or abused. These are, in part, forming our judgements and hence feeding our lack of trust.

In 2009, I worked with a human rights group over a number of months. It wanted to find a way to become more useful to the people it was serving and representing. It didn't take long for this group of promising, dedicated and influential leaders in the organisation to come up against the issue of trust. It really shouldn't have been a surprise that in an organisation dealing with communities where trust had been abused, they themselves faced issues of trust. Over time the group was able to interrogate this issue of trust and found that it actually didn't trust itself to lead. The organisation was trying to do something quite ambitious on a complex issue with no real precedent or road map. A new type of wisdom needed to emerge which was creating uncertainty and fear in the organisation and this leadership group. And as they trusted themselves more and judged themselves and their superiors less, they were suddenly much more courageous, creative and collaborative.

It begins with trusting ourselves to work in a way that may not have many reference points. Our judgements have provided us with reference points in the past—at least they give the illusion of making us think we know where we are. If we trust ourselves and others and seek to be beneficial, actually everything becomes a lot more practical and workable and less theoretical or ideological.

This may provoke certain concerns:

- What happens if I can't be the one who's right?
- What do I do if I am not the one doing everything—what is my use?

- What will happen to my enemies or opponents if I let the
  situation develop the wisdom?

At Social Leadership Australia, one of the things we
regularly hear is how often senior executives are pleasantly
surprised when they allow themselves to trust their people.
What many find is that instead of feeling anxious about the
quality of the work done by others, they actually become
anxious about what their own role will be now that they have
handed over responsibility to others.

This is an opportunity to understand the real nature
of leadership work. Exercising leadership is actually a
deepening—there is no resting or end point. We are constantly
finding ways for the situation to uncover its own wisdom
and that work has no ending. It is kind of an unpacking or
uncovering rather than adding more: a difficult temptation
for people who are used to directing and being the expert.
This is actually great news because it gives us something
challenging and meaningful to do. And we can constantly
push ourselves and find new ways to learn.

This is the road of insight. Insight means to see something new in something that may be old. And we can't be
insightful and judgemental at the same time. This may allow
us to believe in something much more intransient than
our judgements, something that we can really trust—the
potential of people.

If we can give away our investment in being right, we are
finally able to also be more compassionate. Being present
in this way requires more than trust—it requires another
important meta-skill. Myrna Lewis, the deep democracy

practitioner, calls this skill the 'mega-metaskill', one that tempers our passion: neutrality. That's the next chapter.

REFLECTION QUESTIONS

1. Think about a situation in which you are involved which feels 'stuck'.
   a. What judgements have you made about others in the situation?
   b. What judgements have you made about yourself?
   c. If you were to put these aside, how could you actually be of benefit?
2. Who is someone who holds a negative judgement about you? What potential are they not seeing? What could you do to allow them to shift that judgement (that is, how could you benefit their situation—and yours)?

6
Neutrality and passion

Being yourself is a political activity.
Arnold Mindell

PASSION—FOR WHOM?

A number of times so far in this book I have talked about being useful or beneficial to the systems and people we are working with. We do this by being compassionate and allowing people to find their own wisdom—allowing systems to learn. Doing this kind of work and tackling tough issues requires a certain level of energy. If we didn't get fired up about what is happening around us then nothing would ever happen.

An old boss of mine used to say, 'I would rather have people working for me who I need to throw water over than those I need to light fires under.' So would I. I want partners, bosses, colleagues and subordinates with energy and commitment, what we often call passion. Many of the great world leaders we admire have this passion. In South Africa there was no shortage of passion, commitment and energy at the time of Mandela's release. But passion alone would probably have landed South Africa in civil war.

> A different kind of ANC leader could have elected the easier option of tapping into the indignity and hurt black South Africa had endured and channelled it towards violent confrontation. It took a rare wisdom for Mandela to say to his people, 'I understand your anger. But if you are building a new South Africa you ought to be prepared to work with people you don't like.'[1]

I have worked with many dedicated and passionate leaders, people whom I greatly admire. All of these people had to find their way through a number of questions so they didn't end up as martyrs, alienate themselves or burn themselves out:

- How do I separate myself from the issue?
- Is this about me or about moving the issue forward?
- When do I 'let go' or give up?
- How do I stay alive?

These questions do not have definitive answers. We have to work through them and answer them based on who we are and the context we find ourselves in: these questions test the strength of our 'neutrality muscle'.

LONG LIVE THE MARTYRS

Why is it okay to be passionate but not so attractive to be a martyr? Isn't martyrdom just a logical conclusion of being passionate about our view of the way things should be? Most people would answer that everything is a matter of degree; that it is important that people are passionate but that martyrdom is going too far.

I am not so sure. There is something quite alluring about the martyr, whether it is the reviled suicide bomber or the revered Mother Teresa. Martyrs are a fascination. They embody many of what we consider to be positive human traits: dedication, single-mindedness, discipline, industry and faith. Martyrs seemingly put the issue ahead of themselves. They embody passion.

We often hear that conviction is what matters. People may say 'he really believes in what he is doing!' and 'she is so dedicated'. We say people with conviction have integrity. In a way we are seduced by people's passion. But we also seduce them. In popular culture they are the stuff of films and books. From independence fighters to environmental crusaders, we can easily mythologise them and can forgive their many wrongs, or at least conveniently overlook them. We do this because they perform a convenient function for us—as long as we agree with their view. In other circumstances we might label them fanatics or even terrorists.

We need people to hold the issues and represent them strongly; to sound the bell against injustice, inefficiency and danger—people who can disturb the status quo. But does this passion get in the way of exercising leadership? We need to think about how to use all our energies and motivation, our passion, to do benefit in a way that does not lead to a degree of martyrdom that is no longer useful for the issue or ourselves.

PASSION AND IDENTITY

Our passions are linked inextricably to who we are—our identity. Why else would we have so much energy about an issue? Because it is never just about an issue—it's also about us.

> Sheila is the founder of an NGO that supports communities in Kenya to address public health issues. She is a Kenyan herself and studied in Australia, the USA and the UK. She is passionate about what she does. She is also burnt out. Her 2009 board does not seem to share her passion, giving her little support or direction.
>
> She feels she must not fail and this passion is clouding her capability to exercise leadership. There is a lot at stake—more than meets the eye. When she established the organisation, she approached a potential donor who turned down her request for funding. He felt that organisations run by Africans were bound to fail. She is determined to prove him wrong, but her passion is starting to do her and her organisation harm.

This is a particularly emotionally charged example of our identity being inextricably woven into the issue. It can be much more benign than this. For example, it could be how our identity is linked to our profession, which always has us championing a certain perspective in our organisation. Or it could be a core value which triggers us to fight for a certain cause, project or idea.

When so much is at stake it's hard to get perspective: we think 'right' is on our side. And losing or giving up is not an option. We need to be right because, after all, this is about who we are as people. So there is a pride at play here which is less than useful. And we are usually not alone in feeling and reacting in a certain way.

PASSION AND FACTIONS—YOU ARE NOT ALONE

If we look at any adaptive challenge we will see that the people involved are organised into a variety of factions—consciously or unconsciously. In political life things are conveniently labelled. For example, one can come from the centre right of a left wing party. Usually these divisions are not so obvious in other aspects of life and it requires a problem or issue for the factions to surface. In our organisations sometimes these factions are functionally aligned: marketing, production, management or by region. Or they could have more to do with legacy—the old timers vs the young guns. In crises it can be as simple as 'those that are with us and those that are against us'. The deeper into the core of a faction we go, the more we find the pure passion of that faction. At the core are also some other less attractive traits: anger, xenophobia, distrust, selfishness and pride. And of course ego.

Factions love themselves. The faction will build, promote, support and encourage us—almost like a family. Our faction brings us safety and gives us identity. It can be our way of finding voice, particularly for difficult problems. And when we start to lead, we often do so from our faction. The 'love' comes with an expectation that we will deliver benefits, or a win, to the faction. Factions are more than the individuals who are in them—they are a broader view, grouping or alignment which exist independently of the people in the faction.

The greater your passion the more you will be revered and mythologised. Or if you come from an opposing faction, the more you will be reviled. Ask yourself: is 'zeal' a good word or a bad word? It depends on whose name you put next to it and whether you agree with their position or not.

The array of factions that form or become apparent around any leadership issue is a natural part of a human system. They will always exist and are indeed a healthy part of the diversity of the system. Unfortunately, pretty soon we know what each group is going to say before it opens its mouth. We just need to press 'play'. At an organisational level we can usually predict how our meetings will look—who will be lining up behind which particular position. Even in our families we can see familiar patterns or loyalties play out.

As familiar and predictable as the factions may be, they disturb us. The idea that there are people who may see things significantly differently to us can be, at its mildest, quite irritating and confusing. Organisations often make the mistake of trying to make the factions go away by appealing to a common set of values. Sometimes the more fractious a workplace, the more prominent its display of 'core values' (look for them on mouse pads and on posters near the elevators). Often, too, they try to silence the minority faction; those that are out of vogue, irritating or building power.

What's your faction?

Think about a difficult issue in your workplace, a problem that doesn't really seem to go away despite a few attempted quick fixes every now and then. Consider the different 'sides' or points of view around the issue:

- How would you describe the different points of view?
- What is their line of argument?
- What do they value?
- What might they win or lose if there is a change?

Now consider where you stand in this:

- What do you normally stand up for?
- What does your 'voice' sound like?
- What provokes you or pleases you?
- With whom do you normally side?

Now see if you can give these different factions some nicknames. In my workplace some of them would be:

- 'We are all one happy family.'
- 'Things need to change.'
- 'Our clients come first.'

Consider that these factions are natural parts of the system you operate in and that they will always rub against each other whether you are there or not. What does that mean about what you could do differently to make progress?

We will almost always come from a particular faction. This relationship performs a useful service for us. As we provide benefit to that faction it will, in turn, provide services to us, the most important of which are power and protection. These are important in exercising leadership. They also give us a script to follow.

PROBLEMS WITH PASSION: THE DANGERS IN THE FACTIONS

So what's the problem? If we are content with the way things are, there isn't one. The diverse points of view, the passionate leaders who emerge and the various factions on any particular issue are what hold the status quo firmly in place. The competing powers have found a way to make the status quo 'work', like a set of scales finding balance (even if it looks dysfunctional from the outside). Many union–management relationships look like this: both parties hold deeply entrenched views, see each other as the enemy and are beholden to opposing ideologies and constituencies.

The problem arises when we wish to make change, not just negotiate—particularly change that is lasting, change that requires that the system learn. So the convictions we prize and hold dear can be limiting; they are part of the opposing and equal forces maintaining the equilibrium and blocking system learning.

We often think of maintaining our convictions as being courageous. This might not be true. As the American existential psychologist Rollo May puts it, change requires a new kind of courage:

This dialectic relationship between conviction and doubt is characteristic of the highest types of courage ... People who claim to be absolutely convinced that their stand is the only one, are dangerous. Such conviction is the essence not only of dogmatism, but of its more destructive cousin, fanaticism. It blocks off the user from learning new truths, and it is a dead give-away of unconscious doubt. The person then has to double his or her protests in order to quiet not only the opposition, but his or her own unconscious doubts as well.

So whose side do I take when exercising leadership? Can we be fully committed yet open to the idea that we might be wrong? We need to leave ourselves open not only to doubt, but to other factions. In fact we need a new 'side' to be on—one that *really* requires courage.

SIDING WITH THE WHOLE[2]

I am standing in a room with 25 rising middle managers from a large organisation. These 25 have been identified as 'talent': managers who have performed exceptionally and have shown the potential to rise within the organisation. We are talking about what it would mean to exercise leadership in their context.

The group is starting to realise that they have been selected to progress in the organisation, with the intent of making progress for the whole organisation, not just their area. Everyone bought into this at a conceptual level; now the reality is starting to sink in. This generates fear, distrust and confusion. 'But our bosses don't do that!', 'Who will look out for the interests of my area?', 'I will get taken advantage of!' and 'I am happy where I am!'

The conversation is a familiar one. It is one that happens again and again—not only for this organisation but in every system where people are progressing and are being given more systemic responsibility.

Unfortunately, in most organisations, leaders don't progress though this dilemma. They remain part of their faction—whether that faction is a function, ideology, geography or political point of view. This inevitably creates a polarisation—an us and them and a winner and loser. It means we create tools for war and not for peace; for conflict with losers and a nominal winner but not progress for the system.

The work of leadership requires us to be able to work *across* factions and their different values, goals and ideologies. We need people who can think of *the whole*, not just their side.

Shifting our thinking to the whole allows a new type of pride to develop—one that is more useful, lasting and inclusive: *pride for the whole*.

WORKING LIGHTLY

The capability to think of the whole requires a degree of neutrality. Being neutral is an alien concept to most of us because we spend our lives being *non*-neutral. We have loyalties to ideas, habits, philosophies, politics, affiliations and factions. We see neutrality so rarely that when it happens it is truly extraordinary.

It gives us some understanding of why Nelson Mandela is so revered. How was he able to exercise leadership in a way that allowed South Africa to transition from apartheid to an open democracy in the face of almost certain civil war? In story after story of the work of Mandela, from his early meetings with President Botha while still in gaol to the eventual free elections, there is one consistent theme: the numerous factions he dealt with through those complex and dangerous years were met with a determination to benefit the whole. The variety of white factions he met with from the moderate to the extreme all reported being surprised by him: they were amazed that he wasn't fanatical or threatening. In fact he was charming. Indeed, he went out of his way to learn Afrikaans, so he could greet their leaders in their own language.

Somewhere in his gaol term he understood that fighting from his faction (which in the early years at its most extreme advocated 'one settler, one bullet') would end in bloodshed. He resisted the seduction of his own faction *and* the dangers in the opposing factions. This allowed him to partner with the new president, De Klerk, to find creative ways of bridging the seemingly insurmountable gap between white and black South Africans.

Being more neutral allows us to work lightly. It allows us to see that all things are interconnected and dynamic. In our factions we may be attaching ourselves to things that might be the most transient of all: opinions and loyalties. Anyone who has worked in politics knows how quickly these can change.

'The wisdom of children' is a phrase I have often heard when a child is able to see through the situation to what is really happening. This wisdom comes from neutrality;

children have few alliances, baggage or attachments. Their identity is still forming. They can be awake, fresh and curious. Neutrality does not mean forced detachment or an absence of emotion. Nor is it a defence against what is going on around us. It is energetic, alive and perceptive rather than overheated or frozen.

Neutrality may not be for everyone. But if our goal is progress, we can't do without it. And progress in leadership is people understanding and solving their own problems. This is an important philosophical underpinning for the practice of a more neutral way of working. Our ability to be neutral is underpinned by a belief that people, organisations and communities have their own wisdom. And our role is to be neutral enough to bring it out. If we don't believe that, and indeed there will be situations where external wisdom is required, we are going to struggle to be neutral.

FULLY COMMITTED—WORKING NEUTRALLY

The way the word neutrality is commonly used can make it sound quite boring. The neutral gear on my car has the engine running but no motion. Think of neutral countries and we think of Switzerland. Nice watches and a renowned banking sector but I would choose Italy with its drama and passion for my holiday.

But the kind of neutrality we are talking about here is not a passive exercise—a zombie state. It's not about feeling and believing in nothing. It is actually being completely alive and using all our energies, not using the auto-pilot of our well developed views, passions and factional alliances.

It is a mistake to think that neutrality is a cop-out for feeling and participating in what is going on. We are not 'detached'; we are simply not attached to any particular outcome or method apart from progress. There is a difference between being neutral in order to intervene effectively and being detached, not caring or being scared of the action. Being neutral, in fact, allows us to be fully present.

The aim is to be intensely purposeful *and* neutral, so that we can still act in a non-neutral way, but do this from a place of neutrality. That is, we have got the distance we need to see what can benefit the situation and then choose how to act. As Carlos Castaneda explains: 'Feeling important makes one heavy, clumsy and vain. To be a warrior one needs to be light and fluid.'

Can we imagine being passionate from a position of neutrality? Without the self-importance and heaviness?

WORKING WITH THE MIRRORS—PRACTISING NEUTRALITY

I have talked to, observed and worked with many leaders of change over the years and found that there is no one right way to balance our passion and neutrality. We need enough passion to go forward but not so much that we lose our perspective. There is also no easy answer to the accompanying question of when to give up or when to persevere (against the odds). But we can practise and find our own way to be more neutral. The following ideas will help build your neutrality 'muscle' so we can better answer the critical question of *how do we make the greatest benefit for the most people for the longest time?* We can really only answer this question well when we are doing this from as neutral a position as possible.

It is unreasonable to expect that we can be neutral all the time—we are always in some way affected by our surroundings, history and who we are. If we are lucky we will get a few seconds, long enough to make better decisions. The best we can do is try to approach neutrality. I have seen great shifts in how people have been able to benefit their work by making just marginal change in their positions.

If we are to take this challenge to 'become a warrior', to be light and fluid, there are a number of things we can do to build our neutrality muscle. I outline a number of ideas here that can be strengthened by the exercises at the end of the chapter. To explain these ideas I will use the metaphor of mirrors.

One of the installations of Danish-Icelandic artist Olafur Eliasson comprises of mirrors of different size and colour hanging in a room where light is projected onto the mirrors from different angles. As the mirrors turn, they reflect light onto each other and adjoining surfaces. As Olafur puts it, 'the activity becomes more important than the materials' as the space comes to life. If we think of ourselves as a mirror of certain size, shape and colour interacting with other mirrors, light and spaces, we can start to get more of a neutral view. We can get an appreciation of the whole, our impact on it and it on us, of what we are doing when we are trying to exercise leadership.

1. SHINING A LIGHT ON YOUR MIRROR

The first step is awareness and recognition of who we are and what we bring. Let's face it—habits are hard to break. Usually, whether we like it or not we are going to start from a space which is very un-neutral—it will have a certain colour and shape. We behave in patterns that are formed over many years and seem like reflex. The challenge is to be *reflective* and not *reflexive*.

If we are going to work with the whole, we can begin with ourselves. What is your mirror? This includes our politics, social roles, cultural background, and relationship to authority, among other things. Exercise 1 is a useful way to plot this and understand what's coming into the room with you. This is not only what you actually bring into the room but also what others expect you to bring into the room. These expectations can actually be a much more powerful pull on our behaviour than what we consciously do. Sometimes we may be the last person in the room to understand what it is we are doing. For example, I know that my mirror will mean that I usually challenge people in roles of authority and that I am highly sensitive to class. This affects my behaviour and has me acting in ways which everyone else expects and of which I am usually unaware.

2. LOOKING AT WHAT IS REFLECTED

We can begin watching what happens the moment we start working with others (the other mirrors), particularly other factions. Our bodies, mind and speech are great barometers. What sparked my defensiveness? What buttons does your 'enemy' (real or imagined) push? What will always get a rise out of you? People closest to you (and particularly your family) know all these buttons.

These reactions can start to give us a clue to where we may lose our neutrality and go back to reflexive patterns. When we 'lose it' we are back in the fray whether we want to or not. Awareness is the first step of getting some distance. Exercise 2 can help make some of the reflexive patterns more clear.

When we exercise leadership we bring our mirror with our passions, the goals of our faction and a preconceived approach or outcome into the room. If we can practise putting that on hold we can allow all the wisdom in the space to surface—we can put aside our 'material' and focus more on the 'activity'. We often think that if we don't represent our view no one else will. Or that we have the 'right' way of doing things. Generally this is just us being self important or unimaginative: we cannot see that it may not just be us who believes what we believe. Or we may think that everything depends on us.

What we actually need is some space from ourselves, our view and faction. We can start with not taking ourselves too seriously and realising that we are *just one* voice, view or faction in the space. There are a number of visible techniques we can use to gain this space. Exercise 3 has some methods you can use to try build your neutrality muscle. Then there is the further work we can do to get some space from our thoughts, positions and feelings. In my opinion, meditation is one of the most effective tools in learning to be much lighter in our mind and hence our work. Exercise 4 has a suggested meditative practice.

3. HOLDING STEADY WITHOUT BUYING OR SELLING

Sometimes we have a preoccupation with outcomes at the expense of progress. So much so that we are willing to walk away with nothing, safe in the knowledge that we pushed for our outcome rather than allowing an (at first) slower, creative process to take place. Our job is to allow the wisdom to surface and to support this creative process. There will be many temptations to go back to the 'same old-same old'. In response we can harden to protect ourselves. We need to be able to hold steady to the purpose and gently keep working.

In the rough and tumble of the battles of factional life it is easy to forget purpose. We can become obsessed with holding our ground, gaining small wins and looking good. We can become seduced by our faction, other factions and ourselves to divert from our purpose because the work can be hard. A teacher of mine always used to say that to be useful we need to 'never be buying or selling'. If we are working for the whole and trying to make the greatest benefit for the most people for the longest time, we can't be selling our agenda and we can't be buying others' trips. If we think about the meetings we go to we can see this happen on a daily basis. Apart from the official agenda there are always unofficial agendas people are trying to 'sell' to others. It could be a view of the way things are, a project someone is trying to get off the ground or a complaint someone is trying to raise; buying and selling is happening all the time. Our challenge is to not get caught up in this marketplace and remain true to purpose. Exercise 5 will help with that.

4. COMPASSION FOR THE OTHER MIRRORS

If we can see the loyalties, intended outcomes, values and potential losses of people from other factions, we get a larger picture. As individuals, if we start to appreciate their mirrors with its hotspots, preferences and blindspots we can see that, like us, there is a reason they are sitting across from us in the fray. Moreover, we see that all the people we are working with are beholden to their factions. Their faction's expectation is that their view is championed, not compromised. They will need to answer for the work they undertake with us which goes beyond *their* usual positions. Exercise 6 is a useful way to plot the roles in the room.

WHY IS IT SO HARD?

Everyone I spoke to about this chapter either took a deep breath or sighed. 'Good luck,' they seemed to say, 'you will need it.' This is hard. In my experience the exercises at the end of the chapter will bear more fruit than the concepts I have put forward so far in this chapter. Things that are hard need practice. However, I firmly believe that at our base we can be neutral.

But as we practise we inevitably find there are things that get in our way, things that make being neutral counter-intuitive or dangerous.

CHOOSING SAFETY

There is safety in being focused just on our view and danger in moving to a new way of working. We know how to work in our world: how to argue our case convincingly, how to fight with our enemies and what the potential losses are. We are used to the drama and casualties. Sometimes, that can be quite a kick. It can be quite rewarding to see our enemies lose a point. Even losing can sometimes be rewarding: it steels our resolve and allows us to 'circle the wagons'.

Are we committed to the fight or to making progress? Most of us have been in arguments where we realise we are wrong, but would rather keep going than admit it. It can be hard not to look good and be right. If we can't be safe in our 'rightness' then what do we have to hold on to? What is my role if I am not beholden to my view and faction?

Some people face a different danger. Moving out of our safe point of view may mean we come into conflict with others, those that we ignored or didn't even take notice of before. We might find out things about the 'other side' that we don't really want to know—which might challenge our convenient image of them. We have useful phrases to warn us off these dangers of conflict and confusion. We talk about 'hornet's nests' and 'Pandora's boxes'.

> In Greek mythology, Pandora was the first woman on Earth. The gods endowed her with many talents; Aphrodite gave her beauty, Apollo music, Hermes persuasion, and so forth. Hence her name: Pandora, 'all-gifted'.
>
> Pandora had a jar which she was not to open under any circumstance. Driven by curiosity, Pandora opened the jar, and all the evil contained escaped and spread over the earth. Before she could close the lid almost all the contents of the jar had escaped. One thing remained at the bottom: Hope.[3]

The tragedy of the story of Pandora's box might be that we continue to refer to the legend and forget that in addition to the terrible things that came out of the box, at the bottom of the box lay *hope*.

FEAR OF BETRAYAL

Our passion can put us in a gated community. Acting neutrally with the purpose of leading compassionately and wisely means we have to leave our gated community. People back in that community may not be too happy about the places we have travelled to and the things we have learned. They may see our neutrality as a betrayal. We may feel that way about ourselves. It may seem that we have lost our authenticity. So neutrality and thinking of the whole may bring us into conflict with our own faction.

If we expect to come home or still want help and engagement from that community we need to understand this and find a way through these problems. The next chapter looks at authenticity and betrayal in leadership.

AUTHENTIC OR GENEROUS?

I think that the allure of passionate leaders is that we see them as authentic. They are true to their values and firm in what they believe in. The problem is when we have different people trying to exercise leadership who are all authentic to their particular value set and beliefs. How do we bridge the differences and make progress? Who is thinking of the whole system?

An obsession with authenticity can turn us into misers or, at worst, martyrs. And ultimately neither is very generous. It is great to have passion, commitment and energy but when that makes us blind to the whole we are missing the point. We become concerned with being right, winning and (possibly) making sure our enemies lose—we are authentic only to ourselves or our own faction. Building our neutrality muscle allows us to turn our energy and passion into something that benefits everyone: it allows us to be generous with ourselves and others. This kind of authenticity is perhaps a lot more valuable—it is an authentic desire to benefit everyone, the whole.

EXERCISES
EXERCISE 1: YOUR MIRROR
To help you get an understanding of the shape, size and colour of your mirror think about the following questions:

a. What is your relationship to authority? How do you normally work with people in authority or respond to them?

b. What role do you normally occupy in groups? For example, are you a provocateur, peace maker, helper, silent type or do you work behind the scenes?

c. What is your culture and upbringing? How does it manifest when working with others?

d. What is your concept of working together with others? Do you look forward to it or dread it?

e. How is the role you occupy in your family manifesting in group settings?

f. What are the values that drive your work? That is, what is important and what is right for you?

g. Where are you different to others in a group? What is the unique point you have?

h. What are your personal style, skills and strengths?

i. What broader purpose drives you?

j. Where do you get caught? What are your hot buttons and hungers?

EXERCISE 2: THE REFLECTIONS—SEEING OUR VIEW

We usually enter any situation with a fixed view on what is important and what should happen. We can build our neutrality by taking the first step of becoming neutral to our own point of view. Think of a group you work with who generally have a variety of views. They may clash or argue or they may not dare to really talk together about what is going on. Prepare for the next meeting by answering the following questions:

a. What is my belief about the causes of the issues we face?

b. What is my preferred outcome?

c. What opinion would I normally express?

d. What are the views in the room which I think are furthest from mine?

See if you can think of your position as just one in the mix of all positions. It is neither more nor less valid than the others. Maybe give it a nickname.

EXERCISE 3: PUTTING IT ON HOLD

In your next meeting you might want to try to put 'your position' in another chair or let someone else hold on to it. For example, maybe you are always concerned about safety or risk or innovation or finances. Perhaps you champion a particular ideology or take the 'management perspective'. Remember the view is not going anywhere: it exists independently of you. There are different ways you can do this:

a. Don't fulfil the role/position you usually take and see what happens. That will leave you free to work with all the views and roles.

b. Let the group know that you want to be a bit more neutral. For example, 'I know what I would usually say here, but today I was hoping I (or we) could be a bit more neutral.' Almost invariably someone else will occupy your role when you leave it *if* it is useful for the group. Prepare to notice when this happens.

For example, a colleague of mine recently suggested we start interacting with some of our stakeholders in a new way. I was opposed to this idea and expressed it over a number of meetings. Not surprisingly we kept on coming to the same stuck point every time we met, with each position or role becoming more entrenched. Eventually, I expressed my view clearly and then said I was not going to hold it any more to see what would happen. Within minutes someone else who had previously been opposed to me 'took up' my role and began expressing the concerns I had held. This allowed both sides to hear each other's wisdom for the first time, be more fluid and move forward to a different resolution.

EXERCISE 4: BUILDING AWARENESS
Our lives are constantly 'on'. We are pulled in many directions by different people and issues and have lots to do. If we are

going to change gears and see things in a different way it is hard to do this if we have no space where we can be 'in neutral': a space where we can get some distance from the fray and see what is going on. Meditation is a very useful way of doing this. However, it works at a very subtle level. Many people approach meditation expecting that they can 'clear' or 'empty' their mind. This is an impossible task and not very useful anyway. We are not working in 'empty' spaces—this is not the real world we face.

The purpose of meditation is not to stop all the thoughts, ideas and feelings swirling through us; it is to *be aware* of them. This is exactly the skill we need to be able to practise in real life: becoming aware of what is moving through us and others and then seeking to intervene in a useful way. So in meditation we seek to be aware *but not hold*. The mind is an endless source of stuff as it mirrors what happens in the world. We want to build our skill of watching things arise, seeing them and letting them go. We are practising neutrality by trying to become neutral to our own stuff as a starting point.

A warning: meditation does not offer pay-offs in the moment or the 'bliss' that many people expect. A lot of people (including myself) can find meditation quite frustrating—it can seem that meditating actually does not feel restful at all or that even more thoughts and feelings arise than normal. Your head may feel 'crowded' or you may feel impatient. That's all fine. A more useful way to think about meditation is like going to the gym. For me, gyms are unpleasant places full of funny smells and painful work. Most people don't go to the gym to be in the gym. They go to the gym for what happens outside the gym: to feel and look better. It can be useful to think of meditation in the same way—if it feels hard and frustrating you are probably doing some good work. Then watch what happens to the rest of your life when you begin to meditate, how you will slowly have more space in your work.

There are many different meditations one can try. I have chosen one here which is a Buddhist meditation for non-Buddhists. Please find your own if this doesn't work for you.

To prepare
Sit upright in a chair or on a cushion on the floor. The most important thing is that your back is straight. If you are sitting on a chair move slightly away from the back of the chair so that your back is perpendicular to the floor. Have your feet flat on the floor and legs making a right angle—not crossed. Do not sit on a cushion if your knees hurt—meditation is to train the mind, not your knees! Keep your head straight and eyes looking straight ahead. If you are meditating in the morning it is useful to have your eyes slightly above the line of the horizon to wake you up. If not then look slightly below the horizon with your eyelids shut or open. Open your chest and tuck your chin in very slightly. You should feel strong, open and relaxed.

Rainbow light meditation
We sit relaxed and straight, our right hand resting in our left palm and our thumbs touching lightly.

First, we calm the mind. We feel the formless stream of air coming and going at the tips of our noses and let thoughts and noises pass without evaluation.

Then we decide that we want to meditate to experience the mind's richness and gain distance from any disturbing emotions. Not until then can one really help others.

At the heart-level in the centre of our chest, there now appears a tiny rainbow light. Gradually it expands through our body, totally filling it and dissolving all diseases and obstacles on its way. When we can stay with this awareness our body shines like a lamp and light streams in all directions, filling space. It dissolves the suffering of beings everywhere and the world now shines with great meaning and joy. All are in a pure land, full of limitless possibilities. Everything is self-liberating.

We emanate this light for as long as it feels natural.

When we end this meditation, the light returns and absorbs the outer world into open space. It shines into our bodies, which also dissolves and there is now only awareness, with no form, centre or limit.

Then, like a fish jumping from the water, again a world appears. Everything vibrates with meaning, all beings are perfect in essence and our body and speech are tools for benefiting others.

Finally, we wish that the good that just appeared may become limitless and stream out to everybody. That it will remove their suffering and bring them the only lasting joy, the recognition of the nature of mind.

(Reprinted with permission from Diamond Way Buddhism)

EXERCISE 5: HOLDING STEADY WITHOUT BUYING OR SELLING

Jude Stoddart, a long-standing campaigner and practitioner in the equal opportunity and diversity field, told me about a simple reminder that she uses with the people she works with to stay on purpose and not get caught by the variety of agendas in the room.

It is a simple yet challenging reminder of what we are trying to achieve and how we can be useful in the spot we are in right now. She asks herself and others: Why me, why now, why this?

Try asking this question next time you are working within a group struggling to prioritise, facing difficulties or getting lost, or when these things happen to you personally.

EXERCISE 6: LOOKING AT THE OTHER MIRRORS

Think of a group that you are working in where there is a variety of competing interests at play. Similar to Exercise 2, do this exercise for all the other positions in the room. For each of the factions or roles in the room:

a. What is their belief about the causes of the issues we face?
b. What is their preferred outcome?
c. What opinion would they normally express?
d. What are the views in the room which you think are furthest from this view?

After doing this, what new options do you see for working together with these others parties? How does it change how you might behave, from your faction, in this group?

Part 3
Beyond solo—
working with others

7
Betrayal, trust and identity

Mankind intends to survive, and therefore we are committed to following the path of unification resolutely to its goal. This is difficult for human beings, because, till now, our paramount loyalty has been given to fractions of mankind, not to mankind as a whole.

Arnold Toynbee[1]

ACTS OF BETRAYAL

If we aim to exercise leadership and be useful to our organisations and communities, our ability to pursue neutrality is critical. The more neutral we can be, the more likely it is we can see beyond personal and factional interests and focus on making progress for the whole system. But we are not operating as independently as we would like to believe. No one wants their lives to be disrupted or negatively affected. Least of all our own constituents—people from our own 'side' or faction. They, more than anyone, expect our actions to fulfil their expectations. They hope that others will have to change but not them, or that others will have to lose. When we fail those expectations in the name of progress things can become difficult or punishing.

Jenny is an Indigenous woman from Queensland. She has begun collaborating with a group of white leaders from Brisbane to develop a network of civic leaders in Queensland. As their work becomes more visible to Jenny's own people and she begins to learn new ways of operating, she is called to account. Her people are not pleased that she is 'selling out' and working with the enemy. There is a threat of 'shaming': an act where members of her community physically turn their backs on her when she returns home. This is an immensely symbolic and damaging act, aimed to alienate and punish her for her transgressions.

Gavin works in a government institution in Western Australia. In 2004, he was given the task of trying to improve rates of recidivism for a particularly vulnerable client group. His intervention broke new ground and significantly improved the service and outcomes for this client group. This required working in a new way with those clients: one which flew in the face of some significant organisational norms. It meant re-examining the capabilities of staff and clients alike. Most significantly it meant working with these clients in a much more collaborative way. His actions earned him the wrath and mockery of his co-workers. The more success he had, the greater his alienation; at one point he began receiving anonymous calls at home, jeering his attempts to make change.

Kyrstie worked in an Australian professional services firm. The business had been experiencing a prolonged decline. A new division was established to deliver new services and hopefully new revenue streams. This new division was widely disliked by those in power in the traditional business. Kyrstie came from the traditional side of the business but could see how working with the new division would benefit the organisation. She began to partner with people in the new division. At first this only attracted raised eyebrows. When the partnership yielded its first success, she and her new partners organised champagne to celebrate their teamwork. Suddenly, nobody else in the organisation had time to come for a drink. In the corridor, a senior manager from the traditional side of the business told her not to get too excited. His comment of 'it won't last' was more a threat than an observation.

Jenny, Kyrstie and Gavin understood that the answer to their organisational problems meant being able to work across difference and factions. And, indeed, all three were successful. Jenny was able to use her new network and the skills she developed in working with them to better serve her community and organisation. Kyrstie brought in new and badly needed business to her organisation. And Gavin improved client outcomes and, in turn, his organisation's reputation. But being out on the edge can be punishing; it is often seen as a betrayal. This chapter deals with the betrayal that is regularly at the core of exercising leadership.

BETRAYAL IS A DIRTY WORD

Betrayal is an emotionally loaded word, not one that's often used in the context of leadership. It means to violate a trust placed in you. Not surprisingly, the word doesn't appear in the Harvard case studies on leadership and wouldn't sell many books. Betrayal as a part of leading clashes with our fantasies of leadership: committing noble, insightful acts for grateful followers.

I have found in my interviews, conversations and research that when I introduce the word betrayal, it is generally assumed that the betraying is done *to* leaders, not *by* leaders. We can easily talk about the stories of leaders trying to make progress who face a backlash from those who they thought were their allies or followers. For example, the story of Judas who turned against Jesus is one of the Western world's most well-known acts of betrayal. While this kind of betrayal is difficult, it is easier to imagine for those exercising leadership because it is not the leaders who are seen to be doing the betraying. It is much easier to think of the act of betrayal coming from ungrateful, selfish or ignorant followers.

The idea that in fact the *leaders* are doing the betraying is much more confronting. The general assumption is that this must mean that leaders have let their followers down to serve their own interests. This chapter is not about leaders who have abused their position to serve their own selfish interests at the expense of their constituents. I am not focusing on a malevolent type of betrayal where power and position is abused, i.e. corruption. Instead, this chapter explores the idea that in serving the system and working for the whole we will in some way betray our constituents, that this is part of the territory in exercising leadership.

This 'virtuous betrayal'[2] serves a purpose higher than the individual, although it may not be perceived as such.

> I can't give you permission to tell this story in your book. I have already copped so much flak about what I did. They will find out that I told this story and it will happen all over again. This will be like rubbing their noses in it.
>
> Gavin

Gavin, Jenny and Kyrstie are real people. I had to disguise Gavin's name and industry to tell this story. Jenny took a deep breath and thought her name should be put to this—but she understood the ramifications. Kyrstie has moved on from that role. All three have felt what it is like to be punished by their groups and are very careful not to escalate the issues again or return to it needlessly by having their stories publicly retold. In their work they disturbed the natural order of things (or the equilibrium) and were criticised regardless of how dysfunctional that equilibrium was.

There are people to whom we owe our power. They could be a functional group, political party, community or friends and allies. These 'constituents' depend on us to look after their interests and provide security and stability. When we create disequilibrium people are at best confused. They usually end up feeling betrayed if it means you have forced them to see the world differently.

BETRAYAL AS AN ACT OF LOVE

Leading requires embodying the institutional perspective . . . when moments of significant change open gaps between the institutional and personal, betrayal can become inescapable.
James Krantz

If we believe we are genuinely trying to make things better, there is a temptation to reframe this idea of betrayal; it is not a word we comfortably associate with what we are doing. I do not like to think of myself as a betrayer and neither does anyone else. Nor do we want to suffer the consequences of the betrayal—whether we call it that or not. We have a recipe book for how to deal with people who have betrayed us: shame them, exclude them, silence them, punish them or make them pariahs. It's no wonder we want to avoid the word.

I first wrote the story of Northcott (which appears in Chapter 5) in 2006 in a case study for the Australian Graduate School of Management. When I met with Dominic (the central change agent employed by the Department of Housing) recently to talk about his reflections after leaving the department, I asked him whether he would consider the significant progress he made to be a betrayal of the department, which was paying his wages. He told me of a memorable moment when he was asked to tell the story of Northcott at a conference on community development. A person in the audience asked him who he thought he worked for. Without hesitating (and possibly without considering the implications) he said 'the tenants'. When I asked him how he expected the department would respond to that he laughed,

'Well, I knew I would have to prepare myself for the back-lash.' He understood the dangers if his comment got back to the department (which it did) but said, 'I never saw it as an act of betrayal, I saw it as doing what needed to be done.'

When we try to act with neutrality to make progress we *are* doing what needs to be done. But our constituents may have a very different interpretation of 'what needs to be done'. While the department had ambitions to be developing communities, in practice it was possibly only really ready for keeping the bad news stories out of the press, reducing arrears on rent or minimising damage to property. If Dominic's idea of empowering the tenants was the answer, then this is a very different proposition to what the department had in mind. Our constituents may not appreciate you holding them to account for their ambitions, no matter how noble they may sound.

We can see that very quickly leaders can become the 'lightning rod' or scapegoat for those whose expectations they have failed.[3] Australian parliamentarian Peter Garrett was one of those lightning rods. With his shift from protest-rocker (with the rock band Midnight Oil) and environmental crusader to Labor politician, it wasn't long before he was labelled the 'ultimate sell out' by those whose (narrower) interests he represented before entering Parliament and be-coming a minister. Playing on the words of one of Midnight Oil's hits he was asked rhetorically, 'How do you sleep when your cred is burning?' In many ways he faced a no-win situation, with the Opposition party labelling his ministerial decisions hypocritical (when compared to his pre-politics positions) while supporting the decisions he made.

Professional politicians are keenly aware of the risks involved in not meeting their constituents' needs. Most other leaders underestimate the political risks in failing expectations. Either way we don't take these risks in order to be dare-devils. The risk of betrayal is taken because of a commitment to a greater purpose: progress for the system. We can become blind to the risks and consequences of our actions—it doesn't mean we don't pursue the endeavour—but we need to understand the impact for those feeling betrayed and those doing the betraying.

WHAT'S GOING ON FOR PEOPLE—TRADING IN TRUST

Trust begets trust and betrayal begets betrayal.
D & S Reina

To exercise leadership we need some level of authority. Usually we think of that as the formal power we have through the structures we work in—this type of authority is highly dependent on the context. As contexts shift so does our level of authority. In reality what gives us the most leverage in times of change is the informal authority we have. Trust is one of the most important elements of our informal authority; sometimes it is the only authority we have. When we are exercising leadership we are doing that on the basis of trust. Usually we have been given the trust of a functional group, a community, a political constituency or an interest group. Their trust in us is based on us looking after their interests. They may see us as 'one of them'; they expect this loyalty to be reciprocated. As one manager I worked with once put it, his people felt that they 'owned him'.

When this trust is betrayed (or violated) by our leaders we don't react well. We can become angry and frustrated, or we feel abandoned. This can elicit a number of responses. We may be accused of 'selling out' or 'taking blood money', or be encouraged to join 'them' and not come back. This treatment and the sense of betrayal is usually more intense depending on how long people have been part of the system and how much is at stake—which explains why it is often harsher in Indigenous, religious and ethnic communities than it is in mainstream organisational life. The betrayal can also be accentuated when a group feels highly disempowered in the broader system; loyalty to each other may feel like the only thing the group has. The more there is at stake, the greater the trust and hence the greater the betrayal.

In oppressed groups this 'counter-betrayal' can be particularly fierce for those who try to work beyond their own constituency. Just being successful can be seen as a sell out. I have heard many stories of Indigenous leaders in Australia who can't return to their communities any more because they are seen to have been successful by white Australian measures. Similarly, newly arrived Australians who become more 'mainstream' may be called coconuts or bananas (black or yellow on the outside and white on the inside) by their people.

These reactions can seem irrational and toxic. They are anything but irrational, because the betrayal is tapping into the basic survival instincts for either people's personal future in the system or the cohesiveness of the group. Tremendous fear can be generated as familiar patterns of relationships are interrupted and new ones are formed. We have to remember that while we may be working for the whole, transgressing people's trust is *always* personal: it goes to our emotional core

This puts us in a vulnerable spot, one that we would prefer to get out of. Generally there are two responses for those accused of betrayal: hardening or defensive flight.

BETRAYING OUR IDENTITY?

What's your default when you have to face the impact of failing people's expectations? And when trust in you is under threat? Do you back away and try to please people, shoring up old alliances and loyalties? Or do you distance yourself from the emotional fallout and expect people to toughen up? These are the usual two options—but there is another way: one where we actually stand in the fire and take responsibility for both the system and people's journey. This is a harder spot as it can confront the important stories we have about who we are: our identity.

> Greg is a CEO of a mental health provider. The organisation is undergoing some important shifts to better meet its clients' needs and respond to an expansion of their services and impact. Most of Greg's management team have been in the organisation since its inception. They represent the prevailing culture: supportive, friendly and passionate about the work they do. And because of this culture, the organisation has difficulties having the harder

conversations about performance, suitability to roles and accountability. The adaptation Greg has to lead will mean a betrayal of loyalties, the legacy of the organisation and some friendships. He is at a personal crossroads about who he is and what he is willing to bear in the name of progress.

Most commonly, leaders acquiesce to the resistance of their constituents. The costs are usually seen as too high. We back away in shock at the backlash from people, realising we don't have the stomach for the response. The status quo begins to look attractive again, particularly when that means our power won't be challenged. We might realise that the power we thought we had is insufficient or what we have gets taken away. We can soon find out how much, or how little, trust is invested in us.

Moreover, if we have built our position and authority based on being liked, and on charisma and personality, we are dependent on positive feedback from the systems we work in. We might also encounter some unpleasant truths on how dependent we are on certain conditions. Greg, for example, realised his resistance in leading the difficult changes ahead was because he had a fear of being 'too serious and boring'. He wanted to have fun and be liked. He was beginning to see how that may not be possible all the time.

The other response is to harden up in order to face the backlash by turning into a tyrant and pushing through an agenda. In so doing we further break the bonds of trust and possibly create fertile ground for a coup. It might be more subtle than this; we might consciously or subconsciously ignore the troubling reality of people's reactions: we believe people need to 'dry their eyes', 'toughen up' and 'suck it up'.

> Liz was brought in as general manager of a national youth communications agency. She found an organisation that was unsustainable. More worryingly, she perceived that the board that had appointed her provided little strategic direction to the organisation and neglected its role in facing the organisation's problem areas. Following the resignation of the chair of the board, Liz put forward a bolder blueprint for the organisation's governance. The board rejected her proposal and actions and put her firmly 'back in her box'. As she puts it, 'At the time I was acting in what I believed were the organisation's best interests. Looking back I can see that one of the core questions I was raising around the viability of the organisation to continue had been an issue that the board had been unwilling to address. But I acted as if the board wasn't in the picture at all—which was pretty dumb and naive looking back on it. The feedback I got from some board members was they felt steamrolled by me.

Inevitably we come up against our 'important story'. At the point of betrayal, does this important story about who we are—our identity—turn us into steamrollers or doormats? Is there somewhere in between these two extremes of fight or flight which might be more useful for us and the work we are trying to do?

actually felt betrayed by how he had personally been treated by the CEO in the restructure process. The manager had expected that the CEO would look after him personally.

It won't be the same again. We can't go back to the way things were. You will be viewed differently—maybe no longer 'one of the gang', possibly with suspicion and trepidation. On the upside, you may also find new allies you didn't have before. There is a new status quo; we can embrace it, ignore it or run from it. How are we going to live with this new interpretation of who we are?

2. RESPONSIBILITY

Taking responsibility for this new status quo can be daunting. In his work on betrayal, James Krantz puts it this way: we can 'face the consequences or (we can) face our own lonely regression'. This regression can either be the retreat or the hardening discussed earlier. Either way, we are alone and not that useful any more. If instead we embrace the status quo and take responsibility for our part in it we can continue to be useful.

Where to begin? I did this. We can begin with taking responsibility for the losses. Jenny describes it this way:

> I look above me at more senior leaders in Indigenous Australia and see hardened people . . . balls of steel. For me, I believe we can't move on and make change unless I can take personal responsibility for what I have done. I have to be able to say, 'I know I hurt you. What are we going to do to move forward together?' I have to allow

people to name the feelings about me and the situation. In a way I am trying to model the broader responsibility required for a system to solve its own problems.

We need to bring high levels of consciousness to what we are asking people to give up. Not acknowledging people's loss leaves you and those you are working with in a stuck place. They become enraged when loss is either ignored or disavowed. Acknowledging the loss allows some kind of mourning to take place. Jenny's way of doing this was 'to go and sit under a tree' with people from her community and listen. Putting yourself forward as responsible allows people to move on. It also allows people to see that you have some skin in the game: that you are willing to make yourself vulnerable to move forward. This is after all our goal—that people can learn and grow. But there is a fine line here between taking responsibility and becoming the scape goat. This is where the next bit is important.

I have power. Being more neutral is in itself a form of power. While it is useful to pursue neutrality, that doesn't make people feel any better about where they are or about you. Moreover, the act of betrayal makes your psychological rank evident for all to see: you clearly are not that dependent on the approval of others.

It is hard to have a mature and honest relationship to our power and rank. It is uncomfortable to admit that we have power. Most people have been brought up to be smart, caring, competent or happy—not powerful. We are usually wary of those with power and rank; some are downright scary. At a cultural level, particularly in Western countries, we take pride in poking fun at the powerful and self-important. This cautiousness can lead to a form of political correctness about power that leaves us *all* impotent. It makes us feel safe to think we all have the same amounts of power—but it is not the reality. It also means we never grow up.

I work with many powerful people. Yet if I ask them how powerful they think they are they will shift in their seat, avoid the question or significantly underestimate their power. There is nothing quite like our relationship to power and rank: we are attracted to it, people are enraged by it when they don't have it or lose it, we disavow it if we have it, or are clumsy with it. It is rarely acknowledged by people who have it and hence rarely used well.

Power is drawn from the rank a person holds in society. For example:

- you are reading a book on leadership which means you see yourself as being able to exercise some kind of leadership—most people don't;
- you have the rank to feel that you not only have a responsibility for things that happen in the world but that you can make a difference to those things;
- you are reading in English—a language with world rank;
- you are persistent and diligent—you have got this far into the book;
- you have enough awareness of yourself and surroundings to see that you need to develop and have the luxury of being able to do that;

- you are likely to be able to make choices about jobs, education, travel and where to live;
- you probably have choices in your work about direction, control over people and resources and a voice in your organisation.

That puts you in a very, very small minority of people in the world in terms of rank through context, psychological state, social position and possibly spiritual life.[5] Most people don't have any or have very few of these forms of rank. We can either feel uncomfortable with this or we can own it.

But if we don't own it, that doesn't mean others can't see it. We have very sharp and accurate radar for people's power— it's a survival mechanism, after all. Those around us have a much better understanding of our rank than we do. And when we disavow it and act like it's not there, this inflames people. This applies not only when people feel betrayed but in all life's situations. What are we afraid of? I think we are afraid that if we actually *own* our power and its effect on people we are going to become vulnerable ourselves—that we may get attacked or 'taken down' because we have extra power. Probably, what makes us even more afraid is that if we admit we have it then we may have a responsibility to use it. Waking up to your power and rank means doing what may seem counterintuitive: taking responsibility and making yourself vulnerable.

Rebuilding trust is my job. We need to live through the betrayal and rebuild trust. Trust is our bank account—it needs to be refilled so we can go on working with people. Trust takes time to build and is easily lost. There are many small things we do every day that either diminish or increase people's trust in us. Do we deliver on our promises? Are we competent enough to fulfil the technical elements of our role? Are we clear communicators—not ambiguous or sneaky?

In the short term, though, when we are working with betrayal we have a task to create a space where people can move out of being victims. If we can acknowledge that *we did this* and that *we have power* then we can play a role in that. That's what makes the two elements above so important. This means listening to people who feel betrayed and acknowledging what has happened so they can heal and start to move on. It needs to be done by the person who did the betraying or it festers instead of heals. This means:

- listening to those who have lost from the change;
- acknowledging the loss without defensiveness;
- taking responsibility for your role and purpose;
- providing whatever support is necessary (or will be accepted) to support moving on.

This might sound oversimplified. My experience is that the first three are usually enough and can make profound differences for people. And they are unfortunately rarely done. They also represent an added bonus: they give you data about what is problematic about what you are doing. Too often the heat of the situation means we shut down when people are angry at us and don't collect important data to allow successful implementation. Can we partner with the difficult voices, those who feel betrayed by us, rather than run from them?

3. SELF-PRESERVATION

Put yourself in the place of Jenny, Gavin or Kyrstie. You probably don't need to as you have been there yourself. Your faction, constituents, department or people are blaming you for their loss or pending losses. This takes an emotional toll: it is easy to get burnt out, taken out, give up, lose direction or lose momentum. We need some help to keep going and survive to play another day, to allow us to hold steady. How do we stay open rather than close down and isolate ourselves?

What we need are some critical friends—at least one. Our critical friends are more like confidantes than allies. In political life allies have no allegiance to us beyond the issue. They can come and go depending on whether you are serving their interests. They may have just been betrayed by you. Critical friends, on the other hand, are not that interested in the issue—they are interested in you. They can play a number of important roles.

Keeping you sane. A critical friend is a safety valve with which you can vent and test your ideas and observations. They might be the only person you can trust. We all need friends and helpers on the way to support us—although that might be hard to admit.

Keeping you real. There is always a real threat when we are trying to work across interests and factions that we actually do get captured and seduced by the other side. It's highly probable that you will be accused of this anyway. A critical friend can give you some perspective to understand whether you have actually stayed neutral or have just switched sides.

Your critical friend can help you test your purpose and whether you are sticking to it. And whether you have the authority to do what you need to do.

4. CONFLICT AND COLLABORATION

Betrayal means making a break from history. It needs to be large enough to allow a recasting of meanings, configurations and alliances while still honouring the past. To do this requires a reorientation of our thinking to see that the heat that arises when we exercise leadership can be useful—even if it is levelled at us and we are cast as betrayers. It allows the regeneration that the system requires to move forward. As Arnold Mindell puts it, 'conflict between parts is an attempt by the system to know itself' and to allow change. It requires new ways of working to allow 'new pathways of collaboration'. But we need to prepare ourselves so we don't run or harden.

This is the 'big incompetence' we all have. We have never really been taught how to work with others, particularly those who think and feel differently to us. Being able to partner with the dissenting voices in your faction and in the broader system is the key to surviving the backlash against your betrayal.

BETRAYAL AND COMPASSION

If we can survive betrayal we can really help systems advance. It is not easy but it can make us stronger and, ironically, more compassionate. If we can 'stay present to the disapproval or betrayal and let it soften us'[6] we can make progress and come back again to continue to be useful. We may find a new kind of resilience. As Jenny puts it, 'The more I get kicked the stronger I become.' This might sound like hardening up but actually it's not. It's a toughness that has at its heart a way of working with people that really exhibits our love.

This kind of love is on the edge of our competence. That's the next chapter.

REFLECTION QUESTIONS

1. What's the 'important story' you carry about yourself as leader? When under pressure do you back off or harden up? What might be the impact of that?

2. If you think about how your leadership might involve an element of betrayal, what do you feel and think? What changes by viewing it in this way?

3. How do you feel about yourself as an instrument of power? What responsibilities does this imply? What vulnerabilities does that expose?

4. Who can you use as a 'critical friend'?

8
Collaboration, incompetence and vulnerability

Leaders have a deeply ingrained sense that they are supposed to know what is going on and that it is simply unacceptable for them to act as if they do not know. Indeed, part of the image of being a successful leader is putting on 'an air of confident knowledge'. To say 'I don't know' is to go against the norms of what a leader is expected to say.
Leslie Perlow[1]

A CHANGE IN THE GAME

School, university and our first jobs prepare us to do work that is almost entirely technical: applying the skills and knowledge developed and tested by someone else to the work in front of us right now. In the first half of our careers we are not usually given responsibility for the problems with which our system is struggling. We do work that has been done before where the answer is known or knowable. We watch and learn.

In this environment things are seen as independent rather than interdependent. We focus on our area, functional goals or politics. We are part of a faction, department or function. This gives us a rich understanding of a narrow field but not of the totality. We do not understand the interdependency and reciprocity of the different parts of the system. We think we can make progress alone.

Pretty soon we build our skills and experience. This competence allows us to advance: we are given and seek broader horizons and bigger agendas. This promotes most people to the middle of a hierarchy or problem. The way up and through is more complex. This is the domain of the adaptive problems. We have been promoted based on skills and diligence in one domain to a completely different domain, one which requires something different— collaboration. Or we have put ourselves there and find we are in deep water. This is the place where many falter, looking for certainty, quick results and positive feedback.

Of course making progress at a system level needn't be our job. We may not care, feel we have the capability or even see the interconnectedness. But if we want to make change to the things we care about, we need to move beyond our competence, established skills and expectations into a new domain. One where working as an individual or from a certain faction is no longer useful.

This chapter looks at our 'big incompetence'—collaborating with others. Collaboration is where competent, skilled and well-intentioned people struggle. However, it isn't collaboration *per se* that is the problem. Instead, it is the fact that most skilled and successful people don't know how to be *incompetent*: we don't know how to learn something genuinely hard. So instead of focusing on how to collaborate, I will examine what I think is the real difficulty in collaborating: it's us struggling to work from a place of incompetence.

There are some good books on the technical skills of collaborating which are mentioned at the end of the book. All of these techniques have at their core a way of working that we haven't been taught. Our educational environments encourage and reward individual achievement. If we are lucky we can see team work in action in our own department or team. But rarely do we really see people working together across differences in values, culture, interests and function.

So not only don't we know how to do it, we aren't allowed to admit it because incompetence is a dirty word. We believe it's what gets people fired, demoted or keeps them in a dead end job. Instead of admitting we are incompetent, we just don't collaborate. Can we find a new relationship to this word? If we can I think we can start to learn about real leadership, working with others to make progress.

The 'big incompetence' of collaboration means we have to move from the safety of our past successes. Indeed, our successes so far may have become a hindrance.

CURSED BY SUCCESS

Tanya and Richard are in their early 40s. She works for a large corporation and he works for a government department. They are successful, confident and competent. Both are being given increasing responsibility for the tougher issues in their organisations. And both are used to winning and succeeding.

When I first met them they were both stuck.

Richard said he felt 'a weight and pressure to make a contribution. 'I don't want to just jump in like I always do because I know something different is required. But I don't know how to contribute. I attend our executive meetings and don't know what to say any more. I feel a weight and pressure to get it right. I feel I have to say something or I might lose my job.'

I ask Richard when was the last time he struggled to learn something hard. He thinks for a while and says he can't remember a time—most things have been pretty easy for him. I ask him if he really thinks he will lose his job. 'Well, no, not really.'

Tanya explained that she felt 'support has fallen away. I am in an overly responsive space and not sure about all the assumptions I have been carrying around so far in my career. In the past I have met the expectations to conform and, as I stop doing that, I am feeling very vulnerable. I feel I can't do anything from this uncomfortable spot. I have come up against my personal barriers, particularly, my desire to prove myself to others. This desire is starting to feel really toxic—like I am losing my essence as a person. People are noticing how heavy I am becoming in meetings. I was called off-site to do my performance review and thought I was being fired. It blew me away that they thought I was doing a good job.'

Like Tanya and Richard we all reach this learning edge; we have skills, have been successful, want to take responsibility and make progress, yet we hit a wall. We find we have not been prepared to do the more complicated work of making progress—of allowing people and systems to learn and shift together.

The first struggle we face is that we move into territory where we will actually need to learn and, as a result, find ourselves on foreign turf. Our success and skill have given us little practice in feeling incompetent. So when it happens, it is surprising and destabilising. It can be terrifying.

But it's more than just not knowing how to learn: it's the values we have developed and hold dear that make us stuck. Chris Argyris[2] contends there are four basic values that drive us in our work—particularly in 'knowledge' work. They are:

1. To remain in unilateral control—we can only remain in control when both the questions and the answers are clear. The creative process that adaptive problems require means a system needs to learn and create something new. We can facilitate, use our power and support others, but we can't control what will happen.

2. To maximise winning and minimise losing—winning and losing are fine if we are negotiating simple issues or are not interested in continued relationships, however,

we need to ask what does winning and losing mean in problem-solving between different factions and interest? The paradigm doesn't hold in this context.

3. To suppress negative feelings—the pain of learning, betrayal and disappointment are part of leading. We can't avoid the negative feelings that arise in solving difficult issues for us and others.

4. To be as 'rational' as possible—what is considered 'rational' is completely subjective. As we try to get parties with different values and interests to work together, there is no one idea of 'rational' any more (if ever there was). We find everyone has their own 'rational' as there are conflicting values, cultures, attitudes and assumptions involved. In addition, if we are focused on the rational we miss other important data in understanding and solving the problem—how people are feeling, what doubts, hopes and fears they have.

Do these four values sound familiar? These values allow us to stay safe in our current competence and have been useful up until now; they allow many of us to personally progress through a system. But they are impossible to maintain if we also want to make progress for the system rather than just ourselves.

We can't hold these values and tackle complex problems at the same time. We may need to find new ground to stand on that allows us to acknowledge our incompetence. Indeed we may not have a choice: an overwhelming need to be competent can become, as Tanya puts it, quite 'toxic' to us as people. We hit a wall.

HITTING THE WALL

In the past, I have noticed that when I work with people and we discuss incompetence everybody nods, sees the wisdom in the idea of acknowledging our incompetence and can recognise the patterns and values we get stuck in. We 'get it' at an intellectual level but don't really want to feel it. Actually going into and operating from a place of incompetence is a completely different story.

This is the challenge that all of us face: can we really move things forward without having all the answers and without being in total control? And what about all the skills and experiences we already have—what happens to them?

This is the conundrum—learning to unify two opposing roles within us. Inside of us is a Competent Role that we have built over many years and allows us to function on a daily basis and feel safe. And there is also an Incompetent Role that we disavow which feels dangerous and scary. They generate very different feelings and we can understand why one of them doesn't see the light of day very often.

The challenge we face is how to find a union between these two opposing but complementary forces. How can they help each other rather than one killing the other? Because just as the Competent Role wants to bury the Incompetent Role, so can the Incompetent Role debilitate the Competent Role.

Can we find union between the voices of knowing and not knowing? Between failing and succeeding? This 'union' between these different voices is our challenge in being incompetent. It is also our challenge in collaborating.

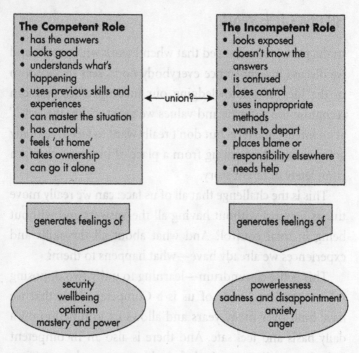

The Competent Role
- has the answers
- looks good
- understands what's happening
- uses previous skills and experiences
- can master the situation
- has control
- feels 'at home'
- takes ownership
- can go it alone

←—union?—→

The Incompetent Role
- looks exposed
- doesn't know the answers
- is confused
- loses control
- uses inappropriate methods
- wants to depart
- places blame or responsibility elsewhere
- needs help

generates feelings of

generates feelings of

security
wellbeing
optimism
mastery and power

powerlessness
sadness and disappointment
anxiety
anger

But what does this union bring? Why bring forth the Incompetent Role within us?

THE FRUITS OF INCOMPETENCE

My incompetence has helped me find my identity. Before it was determined by whomever could seduce me best—to make me feel powerful, liked and certain (and not confused).
Jenny

If we can find a union between our incompetence and competence it is a step towards adaption. Even allowing incompetence to raise its head is an achievement. Most leaders do not let themselves get to a point where they can be incompetent. The more senior we get, the harder it gets to be incompetent as the expectations increase that we will have all the answers. But why is incompetence a good thing—surely we are looking for leaders who are competent?

It's important to be clear about the value and place of incompetence. Feeling incompetent is not a goal, it is a rite of passage to greater learning. Since we haven't been taught to work through conflict, how to lead compassionately, how to betray virtuously or how to collaborate, we need to learn these things. They are not 'downloadable' skills but have to be learnt in the moment. And we *will* get it wrong. So we have to learn again if we aim to be useful.

And the benefits of finding union between these two roles within us are significant. Not just for individuals but more so for the organisations in which we work. Why do most organisations struggle with innovation? I often hear this is a cultural issue. That the organisation is stuck. Or punishes mistakes. Or that there is a 'blame culture'. Yet when I work with individuals from organisations that have these problems I find that they expect the organisation to shift first. This is not where the work begins—it begins with leaders who are brave enough to make mistakes. If we can find a way to allow ourselves to be incompetent we can find:

- *Creativity*—incompetence creates the creative space that is required if we are to make progress. We can't be completely competent and creative at the same time. And this is also what collaboration is—a creative process between people that makes something new through the relationship that wasn't there before.

- *Modelling*—what we hope the people we are leading can do, too, by helping them to realise that they have something to learn. So if we expect others are going to be incompetent for a while then they have to see it is okay for us to be there too. The same applies to collaboration. What people are looking for if they are going to learn or collaborate is some vulnerability in you—because they are going to need to make themselves vulnerable.

- *Disequilibrium*—change comes through disequilibrium. Moving out of the Competent Role is in itself a disruption to the status quo. As one manager said to me with surprise and relief, 'When I stopped acting like I knew what I was doing, other leaders popped up all over the place. I realised they were waiting for the opportunity to empower themselves.'

Seeking unity between the competent and incompetent within us means we make ourselves vulnerable. Maybe vulnerability is what we are really afraid of. We fear we will be judged harshly or disintegrate.

LEANING DOWN THE MOUNTAIN

We sometimes think of the well-adjusted person as having very few problems, while, in fact just the opposite is true . . . the healthy person, the person healthy in body and mind and spirit, is a person with many difficulties. He has a lot of problems, many of which he has deliberately chosen with the sure knowledge that in working toward their solution, he will become more the person he would like to be.

Nicholas Hobbs[3]

Incompetence and collaboration are intertwined. They both show us our strong need for protection and our fear of being vulnerable. We have been taught to be careful about making ourselves vulnerable. And there are good reasons to be careful. Most people have been used or abused by giving too much of themselves away. It happens in the workplace, in our relationships and in our private lives. We build protection because vulnerability is dangerous. We have sustained losses.

If we look around the world at some of the intractable problems we face in our communities, organisations and between nations, we can see just how hard it is to really collaborate. Yet we expect collaboration to be easy—well, as easy as everything we have learned before anyway. It's like expecting to become a master in quantum physics overnight.

We have strong reactions to incompetence as we can feel our very survival is at stake, that our power has been taken away. But the challenge isn't how to deal with less power or to a threat to our power. Rather, it is how do we find balance or union between the forces of competence and incompetence within us? If we can find this balance we can be even more powerful. So it's not about giving up power—it's about giving up protection. As Tanya recalled: 'I saw vulnerability as a negative and dangerous space in the past. I know now that's the state I need to be in. Probably because the days where I thought I could work it all out in my own head are also gone.'

Being incompetent raises new potential losses. Of being wrong, of looking stupid, of losing control or being taken out. But the answer to these potential losses is the opposite of what we expect. It means leaning in.

I learnt to ski quite late in life. Being over six feet tall, with skinny weak legs, a high centre of gravity and questionable balance, I was always going to find it hard. This was a level of incompetence I really wasn't interested in. In my second ski lesson I learnt something that changed everything and kept me thinking long after the lesson was over: when you feel you are losing control or going too fast the only way not to fall is to lean *down* the mountain. At first I had an intellectual rejection of that idea. That can't be right—surely we pull back! And then I had a cellular rejection—I didn't need to think about it—when I started to wobble, my body pulled back anyway. This meant crashing but I knew what that kind of failure looked like. It took me a long time to trust this counterintuitive idea. Yet leaning down the mountain actually made me a better skier. I had to become more vulnerable first.

It is not vulnerability that makes people lose faith in us. There are many other things we do that build faith—keeping true to our word, doing our job, listening to people, showing we care and supporting people when things are hard. Counterintuitively, if we can be vulnerable then this can build even more faith in us because people find in us what we are always searching for in each other: humanity.

UNIFYING THE ROLES: POWER THROUGH VULNERABILITY

There are a number of things we can do to try to arrive safely down the bottom of the mountain. But it is worth remembering that there is no simple way out of our incompetence. We can't be vulnerable and expect some formula will make us feel safe and competent at the same time. We need to sit and work through the range of emotions and difficulties. We need to be human.

I offer below some tips that might be useful. Not as a panacea, but more as a guide that may help people navigate through their own vulnerability and become more resilient.

Welcoming it. How do you react when you feel incompetent? Do you want to hide? Do you cover it up? Do you get angry at the situation? Blame others? It's good to know the signs and use them as a way to recognise that you are on the edge of your competence. What might it take to be vulnerable rather than push it away? If we welcome it then we can start to own it, rather than pushing it onto others. Letting people know you will bear it gives people a sense of safety that it is okay for them to be vulnerable and learn too.

There's also another really good reason to welcome it. If you are trying to make progress on a complex, adaptive issue where progress means people need to collaborate and you are feeling completely competent and invulnerable, there's probably nothing going on. It's a good warning that progress is not really happening. Your incompetence could be a barometer for the group that finally it is on the edge of the real work that's required. And so are you.

Being aware of context. Exercising leadership is not a risk-free endeavour. We cannot wait for the perfect, risk-free moment that, of course, will never come. But leaning down the mountain and jumping off a cliff are two different things. Understanding our context is critical so we don't get abused or punished irreparably. It is good to seek advice from a confidante and really understand how much you can get away with. How much authority you have is also important. Authority power is both a constraint and an opportunity.

Using your power and finding protection. The power and rank we have works like a bank account. This is the time when the formal and informal authority you have can be 'drawn down'. We often underestimate how much power we have and hence underestimate how much incompetence people can bear from us. If we don't have enough power it is useful to have protection from others who do. I know many managers who make sure that they are given protection to do something new. This is important for our survival. You can lose some authority for a short amount of time but we don't want to get de-authorised because people lose faith in us.

Listening. This definitely helps with understanding our context. To quote Tanya, 'When you stop listening and you are incompetent—you are dead.' We need to really hear what is going on in the system—not just so we can learn, but also to work with the disequilibrium that not having the answers has created. Many political analysts have cited this as one of the main reasons for the fall of former Australian prime minister Kevin Rudd. In his government's attempt to tackle complicated problems, he stopped listening and talking. Instead, he relied more and more on a select inner circle, until his party lost faith in his ability to move things forward.

In times of complex change, sometimes authority figures are the only safety people have. If you stop listening and seem incompetent, they will look for safer ground that doesn't involve you. We need to stay close and listen; we may get things wrong. Listening is our assurance that we are not leading everyone off the cliff or that we are creating too great a disequilibrium for people to bear.

Acknowledging the incompetence. Human beings are very good at sniffing out when people don't know what's going on. Acting like you have the answers when you don't just makes people lose even more faith. There is a strong temptation to do this. One manager replayed to me a conversation she had with a subordinate.

Subordinate:	What do you mean you don't know what to do?
CEO:	What if I told you I do know what to do?
Subordinate:	Then I would say you are lying!

Acknowledging the incompetence is the first step in starting to share the work.

Walking the tightrope. This is by far the hardest bit. I have heard this described as 'poise'. There is a certain amount of incompetence that a system can bear. Too little and nothing happens; too much and you look scary or untrustworthy. We need to not fail our role as authority figures to provide protection, direction and order. There needs to be some direction in the mess. Recasting yourself as a facilitator of a discovery process rather than having all the answers is a good place to start. Beyond that, consider how you hold yourself there when you don't know what's going to happen. We need to be vulnerable but not become a train wreck. This is where our neutrality comes into play.

Holding steady. No one may be ready for you to be incompetent all of a sudden, least of all you. Saying 'I don't know' will throw people. Many managers I have seen work with their incompetence find they get cajoled or threatened or face outrage from the people they are working with. We deeply want our leaders to solve our problems and perpetuate the fantasy of the 'omnipotent one'. We have to be able to hold steady, not harden or look for a quick way out. This is one of the hardest things we do as leaders—holding steady against the desire to return to safety.

People are looking for a safe environment in which to take risks; we can wait for the culture to change (and other miracles) or we can create some 'positive deviance' for people to see it can be done. We can show that we can be vulnerable and survive. Moreover, showing we can be vulnerable and incompetent ultimately gives us more power than we had before. Acknowledging and holding it, perversely, gives you power.

So it's not a trade off between power and vulnerability. We can be powerful and vulnerable. Ultimately we find we have less to be scared of.

BUT HOW DO I COLLABORATE?

It may seem like I have deftly avoided the subject of collaboration. It is, after all, very hard and different for each of us. What I need to do with my personality, context, skills and experiences is different to what you may need to do. And it's different every time because who I have to collaborate with is changing all the time too. Indeed I am changing all the time. Collaboration is, after all, about different parties opening themselves up to learn from each other. What that learning will be for each person in that process is different and changes as it progresses. It's hard work and you have to work it out from where you are. Are you ready to be incompetent for a while?

A NEW RELATIONSHIP TO THE DIFFICULTIES WE FACE

We all reach a point in our work when we are faced with a problem but can see that despite our significant skills and experience, our usual responses are just not relevant: we reach the edge of our competence. If we are lucky we might also see that we play a part in 'the mess'.

I am often brought into organisations to work with senior teams having problems with teamwork (or in other words collaboration). Invariably, the team is seen as something that is separate to the individuals in it. 'The team is the problem—but I am okay'. We can see this in more complex issues too. Racism is not my problem because I am not racist. Violence against women is not my problem. Child abuse, the environment; the list goes on. Maybe we say this because we feel helpless. And maybe that helplessness comes from our feelings of incompetence.

At some point we start to see our interconnectedness with the issue we are working on—we are not independent beings floating through space. We mirror humanity's potential and problems. This can sound depressing because it implies that we have a hand in every problem that exists. Of course this is true because every problem happens in humanity and we are humans. Is this depressing or liberating? It depends on our purpose.

If our purpose is to look good it is definitely depressing. If our purpose is to make progress then it is liberating because we don't have to hold up a useless wall any more. We don't need to focus so much on protection of our views, politics and how we look. Instead we can focus on being useful—we can move beyond the trap of our competence with its attachments, preconditions, history and boundaries. And because we are part of humanity and part of the problem we are blessed with all the data we need—we can look inside ourselves to see the limitations, problems, gifts, values, blockages, skills— all the good and the bad are right there. If only we would let ourselves work through the imperfections.

People will be taking their cue from you. Does it seem okay when you do these things—does it look rewarding and inspiring? To quote Jack Nicholson in the film of the same name, this may be 'as good as it gets'. If we open ourselves up to that possibility, we are ready to talk about how to be a real inspiration rather than just fulfilling others' fantasies of perfection and omnipotence. As we become more vulnerable and less protective, we also allow a gift to emerge for us and others—a critical part of leading for the long term. And that gift is joy.

REFLECTION QUESTIONS

1. What are your reactions to the idea of moving into a zone of incompetence? What image of yourself does that challenge?
2. How do you feel about making yourself more vulnerable?
   a. What would you gain?
   b. What would you lose?
   c. What are the risks?
   d. What protection could you draw on?
3. What would 'leaning down the mountain' look like for you?

9
Joy, gratitude and inspiration

Service which is rendered without joy helps neither the servant nor the served. But all other pleasures and possessions pale into nothingness before service which is rendered in a spirit of joy.
Mohandas Gandhi

Joy is the holy fire that keeps our purpose warm and our intelligence aglow.
Helen Keller

THE DIFFICULTY WITH DIFFICULTIES

In trying to exercise leadership it is easy to become trapped in problems and difficulties. We want to make a difference and just knowing and understanding what's going on can be distressing. Seeing that people are being treated poorly and suffering, that our organisation is stuck or lost, or that our environment is under threat is hard enough in itself.

154

Then there's doing something about those problems and what comes with that: getting attacked, being misunderstood, not knowing the answer, dealing with loss (yours and others') and feeling doubt. And that's the exciting part! It is also banal, surviving the relentless trivialities—the work avoidance, bureaucracy, procrastination and prevarication. It can seem there are meetings, committees, processes and protocols specifically designed to make sure we don't make progress. Time slides by and we feel like we are getting nowhere. I often hear the words jaded, tired, confused, betrayed and frustrated from people trying to make progress.

We might start blaming ourselves and feeling inadequate. Or we start to blame the people we are working with. They are not smart enough, are untrustworthy, selfish or out to get you. The world can quickly become a battle. I meet many scarred and weary 'warriors' in my travels.

If our work is sucking the joy out of us, we have fallen into a serious, and common, trap. It is a noble pursuit to exercise leadership: to make the world a better place. Our challenge is to use our curiosity, passion and goodwill in an inspiring, sustainable and joyous way.

THE PLACE OF JOY IN LEADERSHIP

It is interesting that the word joy so rarely surfaces in the context of leadership. Surely joy is the whole point. If joy means to gladden, excite, exult, cause happiness and enjoy, then it seems we have forgotten something. We have got lost in the difficulties, maybe purposefully.

The conversations in our workplaces can be less than inspiring. If you ask someone how they are going they usually reply with 'busy' or launch into what's unsatisfactory in their work or life. Have we glorified difficulties and pain? Is this how we prove our worth? Do we make ourselves vulnerable to jealousy or backlash by talking about the positive things in our work and life? Is the misery safe?

When I begin talking about joy in our work, I find there is usually a sense of relief. It seems we haven't allowed a space for us to actually enjoy or be pleased with our work—for us to be getting something out of our efforts. I see a guilty pleasure in people's eyes. Can this be true? Are we allowed to have fun? Be happy? We worry that we will be punished or not taken seriously.

There is an important truth inside this concern. It is right to be worried about disconnecting from the difficulties and pain in the world through some kind of self-indulgent positivist trip or overly optimistic philosophy. As Pema Chödrön writes:

> The near enemy of joyfulness is overexcitement. We can churn ourselves into a manic state and mistake riding high above the sorrows of the world for unconditional joy. Again, instead of connecting us with others, this separates us. Authentic joy is not a euphoric state or a feeling of being high. Rather, it is a state of appreciation that allows us to participate fully in our lives. We train in rejoicing in the good fortune of self and others.

There is a challenge and paradox in being joyous because so far we have thought of this as an 'either/or' problem. We either fully understand the problems and pain *or* we are joyous, light and happy. The goal is to care, understand, feel *and* be joyous. We have become quite good at leaving our joyous side at home or in our private lives. Or maybe we have taken our work so seriously that our private lives have lost their joy too.

And if you are worried about this sounding self-indulgent, there's more to it than what *we* get out of being joyful in our work. This is actually the most important bit—it's our role as an inspiration to others that makes joy much more than us living fulfilled and happy lives. Potential collaborators and followers are watching us for a cue to work with us. How does it look?

REAL INSPIRATION

I have worked for and with many smart and committed people over the last twenty years. As I reflect on some of those relationships now, there are very few for whom I would be willing to take a risk or make myself vulnerable. Sometimes it's a question of trust. When we don't feel our leaders represent useful values or don't have the competence to do the job, then we can't feel trust. But there's more to it than competence and values.

Competence is a given. Useful values are a given. We can have all that and still be uninspiring. People might be in awe or admire you—but that doesn't mean they want to work with you or for you or emulate you.

In 1992, I joined the Sydney offices of Wilhelmsen Line, a Norwegian shipping firm. Five years before my arrival, the organisation had gone through the most momentous and horrific event in its history. A plane carrying 50 employees, including the CEO and the entire senior management team, had crashed, killing all on board. The plane had been charted to fly from Oslo to Hamburg for a ship-naming ceremony. The employees on board had 'won' the privilege to take the trip by having their names drawn in a lottery. Those with more seniority had their chances favourably weighted in the lottery and as a consequence most on the flight had long service with Wilhelmsen.

Six months after the tragedy, Ingar Skaug was appointed as the new CEO. A native Norwegian, he left a role as Norwegian head of Scandinavian Airlines. Needless to say he faced significant challenges. Not only was the organisation still grieving and missing a large swathe of talent and corporate knowledge, but the business had serious problems. He inherited a top-down, command and control culture, one where risk-taking was limited and change was very slow. In addition he had no experience in the shipping industry and was used to working in a climate of much faster cycles. Nonetheless, he managed to lead an organisation that navigated these difficulties to make Wilhelmsen a leader in its market segment, generate extraordinary profits for many years and create a culture of high loyalty and commitment.

I met Ingar many times in my seven year employment at Wilhelmsen. The longest time I spent with him was after a promotion to a management role where I had responsibility for our Asian trade lanes from Australasia. My more fleeting experiences over the years were confirmed on a day I spent with him in Sydney. He carried a significant responsibility for what had happened and the immediate challenges the organisation faced. He brought tremendous focus, weight and consideration to these problems. Yet he was light and positive and interested in everyone. He wasn't particularly charismatic. After our client visits he closed the door of my office and asked me if he could give me some feedback. He told me some uncomfortable truths about my behaviour that were getting in the way of my work. The lightness he brought to that broke my pretty strong defences at the time and I was actually able to hear what he had to say.

This was the first time in my life where I thought that senior management actually looked like something worth aspiring to. I don't know all the other things he did or didn't do. I do know he made some questionable decisions—though it didn't change his impact and inspiration. Of course he was imperfect and there are other people in the organisation who would not have felt the same way as me. And he didn't do it alone. But I am left with the impact he had on me.

Sometimes it is only us holding people through difficult times, where the future is uncertain, people are experiencing loss and doubt, and we can't make any promises. Or those promises are not meaningful or believable. At moments like these people are taking their cue from us. What is the 'promise' we are offering? Will it be a miserable ride or will there be something I can look forward to? Whether we like it or not we are being watched. I talk to many people who have realised how the mood in the whole office can shift based on how managers are feeling on any given day.

And unfortunately the more difficult the cause or challenge, the less inspiring people can be. It is sad that some of our toughest problems attract such miserable people. I know this sounds harsh, as the issues are depressing and infuriating. Yet we have a duty to find a way to attract people to join the cause—not scare them away. Who wants to work with people who are self-righteous, angry, depressing or debilitating? If we want people to come on board it needs to look like a worthwhile experience. Nobody is coming if it looks painful and unhappy. They will happily let you take that trip alone.

If we are looking for collaborators and partners, we need to give them some kind of reassurance: 'Yes, it might be hard and difficult but you look like you are having an okay time. It looks manageable and maybe even good for you to do this.' We want leaders who would also make good neighbours, not ones who scare us, make us feel unworthy or uncommitted.

But joy doesn't just inspire, it frees us up; it allows us to be light and fluid, and in turn helps us to better exercise leadership. Joy and exercising leadership are not mutually exclusive—they are essential partners. Joy gives us the freedom to take people further, to do harder work, not only because you will have more supporters but also because it is not as tiring.

Maybe we already understand this; maybe we have always known that being an inspiration is actually part of leadership. Yet thinking of ourselves in this way makes many people feel uncomfortable. Perhaps we are scared that we will seem arrogant. I think that's an easy defence. If we really take ourselves seriously as an inspiration, then that is a big responsibility—not an ego trip. It manifests very differently to the pride and blown up ego we are scared of.

Of course it is good to be fearful of getting over-confident and putting our personal agendas above making progress for the whole. A good way to know if we are keeping ourselves down to earth is how willing we are for people to see we are human and flawed and still trying. This 'joyous vulnerability' might actually be the greatest inspiration we can give. If people can see we are not perfect but are willing to take responsibility, that we use our power and that it looks like a positive thing to do for you as a person, then they might just lend a hand.

FINDING JOY, BEING GRATEFUL

So how do we awaken and strengthen the joy in us as leaders? How do we use that joy to be an inspiration for others? These questions are not that easy to answer—we can't just 'turn it on'. But there is a place to start—with gratitude. The Australian philosopher Tony Coady talks about gratitude in this way:

> The capacity for gratitude and for expressing it is an impor-
> tant element in a good life, and those who lack it impoverish
> themselves and others. In a secondary, though very important
> sense, one can be grateful for life itself, or for the way one's life
> has gone, or for certain aspects of it, or for the environment
> one lives in, even where there is no person who has done you
> the service.[1]

When I think about some of the leaders who have inspired me, whom I have either known personally or observed from afar, they have all demonstrated an unmistakable gratitude for their position and its opportunities, even those who seem to have little for which to be grateful.

There are a number of things we have to be grateful for. If we can practise returning to these things in our work, we have the opportunity to refresh the joy that is already within us. It is always there—we just have to keep on bringing ourselves back to our basic nature. Here are three things that can help us refresh.

The personal opportunity. We are incredibly fortunate to be able to exercise leadership at all. Having sufficient capacity, competence, power and awareness to try and benefit the situation is in itself a reason to be grateful. I will go further and call it a blessing. Maybe the only thing we can have gratitude for, particularly those of us working in very difficult situations, is the fact that we are there; that we can do that work. And all the other things in life that allows us to exploit this opportunity. If we have some kind of stability through income, shelter, regular meals and supportive family, friends or colleagues, then we have even more for which to be grateful. Not only are we lucky enough to have these things but we also have the presence and space to think about our efforts and try to improve them.

The moment. There are many conditions that need to come together to make a change possible. Having the external conditions where there is sufficient readiness and urgency to attempt change is rare. The proportion of human history where we have been able to work on gender equality, the welfare of children, the ethics of corporations and the responsibility of governments is actually very small. This is important to remember, particularly for those who are working on very painful issues. It can help to think of the people whose lives we are trying to improve—particularly if they have been badly hurt. We can have gratitude that they are finally in a position where they can try to move on and heal and we have played some beneficial role.

The people. Our collaborators, allies, followers and even enemies can be a gift. These are people who share our journey and are part of our work. Even our enemies are useful in helping us grow and alerting us to our blindspots. Unfortunately, we rarely see gratitude expressed to these people. This is a waste because it is such an easy gift to give that has great payback for the people who are shown gratitude and for those giving it. We all need to be appreciated. That's actually why most people end up leaving their jobs. And it's not something we can ask for. If you have to ask for it, it's too late and has no meaning—unlike more money or a promotion.

We know what being ungrateful looks like—people in positions of power who always seem to be unhappy, wanting more and unappreciative of their role, their opportunities and the people who work for and with them. The legendary, and now infamous, Wall Street financier Michael Milken, who made billions in the 1980s, exemplifies this problem. In 1989 he was indicted for 98 counts of racketeering and securities fraud. But at his peak he was a Wall Street legend with billions of dollars of assets and immense sway in the financial markets. Some of his colleagues and acquaintances talked about what he was like at his peak: 'Nothing is good enough for Michael. He is the most unhappy person I know. He never has enough.' And, 'There seems to be less and less joy in Milken—something that had been part of him in the early years—and more compulsion.'

We can open the business pages almost every day and see the latest examples of the ungrateful. Or read the celebrity news. We might see it in ourselves. This leads to only one place: we soon find that we are always in bad company, surrounded by problems or alone. Ultimately, to quote a teacher of mine, we wonder why we don't harvest apples when we have only planted cactuses.

But why is it so hard to feel gratitude? Why do so many of us often find ourselves complaining, unjoyous and setting a poor example? Why is it so hard to reach what Pema Chödrön talked about in the earlier quote, that 'state of appreciation that allows us to participate fully in our lives'? How can we 'train in rejoicing in the good fortune of self and others'?

I think we have been sold a line that we can have pleasure without difficulties. So we are waiting for things to get better—to be perfect. And this hope for perfection finds a good ally in our consumer society; we are always being told that we need something else. We can't wait for things to get better before we are joyous. We will be waiting a long time. Being grateful is a good antidote to these problems. We might start to see possibilities and potential while acknowledging the problems and pain.

Being grateful does something else that is really important: it brings us into the present. Too often in exercising leadership we are either stuck in the past or planning for the future. While we need to understand what has happened in the past, this is just data—and subjective data at that. We need to think about the future—what we desire—but these are just plans. The potential for leadership exists right now in every single moment. This is how we can really benefit the situation.

What would happen to us and others if we could come into the spaces we are working in, without history or desire, and just seek to benefit? How could we be more effective and joyous for ourselves and by implication inspiring for others? Think about your meetings, your work dynamic, your issues/challenges, home life. What would shift?

LEGACY AND HOPE

The world is in constant flux. Yet we have a desire to make some kind of lasting impact. If we want to make a difference, the most significant thing we can leave behind is inspiration. This is what people like Martin Luther King, Nelson Mandela and Rosa Parks leave behind.

In an ocean that is constantly shifting we seek to be the solid rock not disturbed by the waves of life. This rock is the inspiration we can all be to others: that there is hope that we can transform difficulties and pain into joy and hope. This is a fortunate responsibility.

If we grow into this responsibility, we might understand that one day others may think of us and see it is possible to do hard work and have a light life. They might see there is hope—not only for the problems that we face but also for us as leaders.

REFLECTION QUESTIONS

1. What would change about the situation you are working in if you were able to be more joyous?
2. What do you have to be grateful for?
   a. In the opportunity you have?
   b. In the moment you are working?
   c. From the people you are working with?
3. What would shift if you think of yourself as an inspiration to others? How does it feel to think of yourself that way?

10
The teacher in hopelessness

It is taken as a truism that hope is essential to life. What would it be to have no hopes, to believe that things only get worse, to expect failure and anticipate defeat?
A.C. Grayling[1]

We know that all is impermanent; we know that everything wears out. Although we can buy this intellectually, emotionally we have a deep rooted aversion to it.
Pema Chödrön[2]

THE INCONVENIENT VOICE

Inevitably, in facing the world and exercising leadership we may encounter a voice in us, our communities and organisations that we don't want to hear. It is an inconvenient voice—a voice that feels and expresses the hopelessness of the work we face.

An Indigenous elder talks about his hopes for Australia. He has been fighting for recognition and change for Indigenous Australians his whole life. As he reaches the last quarter of his life he shares with me his feelings of hopelessness. He wonders if it will all be lost for his grandchildren.

Twenty senior executives from a corporation are in an argument about the plight of the organisation. The room is evenly divided. One half believes it is hopeless trying to change the culture—they may as well just leave. The other half thinks it is worth trying and it is their responsibility to make an attempt.

A federal politician reflects on his frustration with the outcomes from the Copenhagen Climate Conference in 2009. He has been a long-term campaigner for green issues and is now feeling tired, angry and lost.

We would like to act like hopelessness is not there within us or in our outside world. But we are surrounded by undeniable evidence. We are polluting our environment, wars continue and hunger affects millions if not billions. In my community child abuse and violent crime seems immutable. What are we to think when prison populations are rising and schools erect higher fences?

I look at myself and at one point need to admit that I am never going to reach the stage where I have got it all together: none of us are. At any rate old age, sickness and death are unavoidable. All my work may well be undone by circumstances or other people. One could say this is a particularly dark view—even a nihilistic one. Maybe it is just an inconvenient view: one that most people, systems and institutions struggle with.

What do these philosophical questions have to do with leadership? Ultimately, leadership *is* a philosophical journey. We inevitably find ourselves facing inconvenient questions of purpose and meaning. When they turn up they can be frustrating, confusing or debilitating. This is part of the territory in attempting to understand our world and make progress.

THE TYRANNY OF HOPE

> *A leader is a trader in hope.*
> Napoleon Bonaparte

In recent times one politician has used hope as a central idea to win a pre-selection and election from a seemingly unwinnable spot. Hope featured prominently in not only the campaigns of Barack Obama but also the books he authored, the second titled *The Audacity of Hope*. In his presidential acceptance speech in Chicago on November 5, 2008 he returned once again to hope as one of the central ideas in his campaign: 'It's the answer that led those who have been told for so long by so many to be cynical, and fearful, and doubtful of what we can achieve to put their hands on the arc of history and bend it once more toward the hope of a better day.'

President Obama follows in the footsteps of many other renowned leaders of our time. When Martin Luther King gave his famous 'I have a dream' public speech at the Lincoln

Memorial on August 28, 1963 he raised the hopes of black and white Americans alike:

> I have a dream that one day this nation will rise up and live out the true meaning of its creed: 'We hold these truths to be self-evident, that all men are created equal.'
>
> I have a dream that one day on the red hills of Georgia, the sons of former slaves and the sons of former slave owners will be able to sit down together at the table of brotherhood.
>
> I have a dream that one day even the state of Mississippi, a state sweltering with the heat of injustice, sweltering with the heat of oppression, will be transformed into an oasis of freedom and justice.
>
> I have a dream that my four little children will one day live in a nation where they will not be judged by the color of their skin but by the content of their character.
>
> I have a dream today!

These words continue to inspire people today. They touch something inside us which yearns for progress and an end to difficulties and pain. We all hope for many things—not just those exercising leadership. We hope for peace, justice, equality, freedom and security. At a day-to-day level we hope for safer communities, a good future for our children and happy, healthy lives. For ourselves we may hope for forgiveness, salvation or enlightenment.

This makes hope a valuable currency in leadership. The noisy politics of human systems values hope above most else: it is the promise behind change. Hope has been used to mobilise and inspire people across the world. It is a comfort in bad and painful times and an impetus to improvement when times are good. Our hopes (and corresponding fears) are easy to tune into and hear and are hence central to religion, popular culture and politics alike: hope is easily tapped by those seeking power. It frames the promises that we make and the power we receive. And of course it can be exploited. We can elevate people to positions of authority because they have fulfilled a fantasy that they can fill our hopes. Or that they can allay our fears.

Using hope and fear as routes to gaining and maintaining power is neither good nor bad in itself. It depends on our motivation. What is more important here, and the focus of this chapter, is how the 'tyranny of hope' can affect the work we have to do. Understandably and perhaps self-evidently, most people trying to make progress have a hope that things will improve. Or a commensurate fear that things won't improve or may even regress. These hopes and fears provide most leaders with the energy and focus to do their work, to sustain and direct it. And hope, particularly, is seen as a positive energy—one that we need not only as leaders but also an energy we require as a society.

I would say that facing into hopelessness is at best counter-cultural. It is difficult to really face the way things are. But like many difficult or unpleasant ideas maybe there is something we can learn from hopelessness—maybe we lose something by disavowing it.

THE JAWS OF EGO

Many years ago I met a Tibetan Buddhist teacher, Sogyal Rinpoche, the renowned author of the *The Tibetan Book of*

Living and Dying. He was giving a lecture at the Australian Graduate School of Management and I asked him a question about fear. In the enigmatic and mysterious style typical of so many spiritual teachers he replied, 'Hope and fear are the jaws of ego' and then moved on to the next question. I pondered this answer. I could understand how fear is a problematic manifestation of our ego. But hope? Surely hope is okay?

Later I realised that what he was trying to say was that hope and fear are two sides of the same coin. What I hope takes me away from what I fear. What I fear is that my hopes are not fulfilled or lost. As I try to live a purposeful life I find myself unintentionally using these words less and less. I can see how dwelling on our hopes and fears means we lose something because they:

- *Take us out of the present.* We fear and hope for things that will happen to us in the future. Or we hope or fear for a return to some past set of conditions.
- *Create an attachment to certain outcomes.* We can be trapped into 'vain pursuits' where we are chasing what we think is right or sounds good to others rather than checking out the real and possibly difficult work that needs to be done.
- *Can debilitate us.* When our hopes are not realised or we realise the insurmountable difficulties and odds of success we may give up. When our fantasies are challenged in the face of real life it is hard to move on.
- *Stop us learning.* Shunning the hopelessness and difficulties in our world takes us away from learning how to deal with them. If we could really hear and see the problems we

face maybe we wouldn't need to be so hopeful—we might learn how to respond usefully.

Let's not discard hope just yet, but put it on hold for a moment so we can hear what a less convenient and less inspiring voice has to teach us.

CAN HOPELESSNESS BE A TEACHER?

If hopelessness is a living part of my reality, what does it offer me as a teacher that other things don't? What does it offer that love, joy, grace and beauty can't give me?

Hopelessness can teach us about pain. People are suffering every day. And we suffer knowing that other people suffer. Our consumer society presents many quick remedies for pain and difficulties in our lives. We can camouflage our decay with Botox and allay our anxieties or depression with Prozac. Institutions, from charities to welfare states, can make us feel that those who are suffering may have their pain allayed. But we can't lead and minimise pain and difficulties at the same time. If we do that we are either in denial or deluded.

Hopelessness can teach us about acceptance. I will never have it all together to respond perfectly to the challenges I face. The world will never sort itself out. If I can begin to accept that, then maybe I can get to work and put my judgements on the way things should be on hold.

Hopelessness can teach us about being humble. The hopelessness of the global challenge can help us be humble by putting an end to our dreams of being superheroes and saints. Maybe we don't need any more saviours; many just seem to make things worse in the long run anyway. Settling into the way things are brings us back to earth and gives us a more realistic sense of both the pay-offs we can expect and how 'right' we can expect to feel. If I could be humble enough to see that I too am impatient with my children, am not always kind and lose my temper, then maybe I could be a good ally rather than a judge to all the people I deal with.

Hopelessness can teach us about being present. What use are my hopes if they don't change what I am doing in the moment? When we look beyond ourselves we find many things to do. But when it becomes tied up with hope and fear we move out of the present and into the future or past. Actually all our work is in the present. Leadership can only be in the present. The reality of the situations that we face 'nails' us to this moment. It doesn't mean our plans and hopes aren't useful, but they are useless if they don't allow us to shift what is happening right now. Dreams of utopia don't help anyone.

Hopelessness can teach us about purpose. The reality of the situations we face can bring us back to our purpose. Hopes can sometimes stand in our way and make us forget what we are meant to achieve.

The teacher of hopelessness might allow us to wake up to ourselves and our surroundings, to see things as they are. We have an opportunity to grow up. This is good news because we need more leaders who are not afraid of the way things are, have their feet on the ground and can take action.

GROWING UP—MORE MEANING FEWER PROJECTS

Sometimes we feel that one individual's action is very insignificant.
But the movement of the society, community or group of people
means joining individuals. Society means a collection of individuals,
so that initiative must come from individuals. Unless each
individual develops a sense of responsibility, the whole community
cannot move. So therefore, it is very essential that we should not feel
that individual effort is meaningless—you should not feel that way.
We should make an effort.

His Holiness the Dalai Lama

In our work at Social Leadership Australia we meet a great many leaders and organisations trying to make progress. This is a privilege and a curse. We encounter the hopes of many people and the corresponding hopelessness in their situation. We all respond in different ways to this. Personally, I find myself cycling into a state of hopelessness about the work we do every three months or so. I see many others share these feelings (although few admit it). It can escalate into despair and profound loneliness. This can feel overwhelming. I was recently sharing my feelings with my colleague and long-time friend Robbie. When I finished he said, 'Of course it's hopeless, but that doesn't mean it's not meaningful.'

Like all the people I work with and for, I face the same dilemma: how can I have a meaningful life? The idea that our efforts have no meaning can be unbearable. Ultimately our work is filling a basic need to live a life that is purposeful. Exercising leadership is some people's way of living a meaningful life. Robbie's comments were not meant to cheer me up or give me hope. They actually helped me wake up and grow up a little bit. It called to mind a passage from Peter Singer's book *How Are We To Live?*:

> Now someone might say: 'What good have you done? In a thousand years these people will all be dead, and their children and their grandchildren as well, and nothing you have done will make any difference'. That may be true, or it may be false . . . We simply cannot tell. We should not, however, think of our efforts as wasted unless they endure forever, or even for a very long time. If we regard time as a fourth dimension, then we can think of the universe . . . as a four dimensional entity. We can then make that four-dimensional world a better place by causing there to be less pointless suffering in one particular place, at one particular time, than there would otherwise have been. As long as we do not thereby increase suffering at some other place or time, or cause any other comparable loss of value, we will have had a positive effect on the universe.[3]

I reflect on Singer's ideas when I think of my hopes for my own children. Like many parents I find myself thinking about their future: the world they will inherit, the dangers for them, their loves and lovers, their work and happiness. It is hard not to hope. But I also know that I can't control any of these things. My role as a parent is in many ways hopeless. They may be happy or they may not. They may be a friend as I age and die, or they could become estranged from me. These hopes and fears only fill me with worry, sadness or unrealistic expectations. I become attached to a future I cannot in any way conceive and only partially influence.

The joy of our relationship and the usefulness I have as a parent (and leader) for my children is all here—right now. The only way I can be useful to them is if I don't get caught in the 'jaws of ego' myself, but rather focus on being beneficial and loving. At any rate, my children, like the world, are not interested in the past or the future. They are here in the present and seeking my presence. So is the world.

So perhaps I can stop thinking of my children and the world's problems as projects to fix and instead start thinking about my purpose and role. Perhaps I can't fix very much or make progress on many problems. Perhaps my efforts will be undone. Ultimately, there is 'no cure for hot and cold', for joy and pain, for love and hate. Carpenters do not lament the fact that eventually one day their furniture will break and decay. There will be more carpenters and more timber. Police do not expect crime to stop because of their efforts. There will be more crime, criminals and police. Perhaps in exercising leadership we are taking a role in a story that is much larger than us: this is the story of the ongoing battle to both relieve others' difficulties and pain and to reach our potential as human beings. Our role is one that is required to maintain the balance that the system requires to function and survive. We are holders of a tradition of unending work that can positively impact every one we touch right here and now.

I don't believe hope has no value. Hope tells us about what we think is important and right in the world. It connects us to what we have in common as human beings. Maybe if we can also understand the hopelessness of our situation we can manifest what we want to see in the world right now where it is needed. Perhaps that will allow us to hold our hopes more lightly, to be more neutral. In any case, we don't make this progress through hope—we make it through love. Love is the reason why embracing hopelessness doesn't turn into nihilism.

Love in leadership is the next, and final, chapter.

11
Leadership and love

People attempt love as climbers attempt Everest; they scramble along, and end by camping in the foothills, or half-way up, wherever their compromises leave them. Some get high enough to see the view, which we know is magnificent, for we have all glimpsed it in dreams.
A.C. Grayling

WHAT DOES THE WORLD NEED NOW?

Ultimately leadership is a flawed and limited word to describe what the world really needs. In the way leadership is talked about in daily life, it clearly has little real power, compassion or wisdom. At any rate there is rarely enough of these things to facilitate useful change. Our focus on leaders (rather than leading) and the fantasies we have about leadership means we neglect the whole purpose of leading: growth. And things grow with love. This base, love, is not only the grounding motivation for leading, it is the process, measurement and goal. It carries with it the universal responsibility for fellow human beings that leadership does not. This is a responsibility to make a positive impact by bringing happiness and reducing suffering for all of us.

Love and leadership are not often spoken about in the same sentence. In my work with thousands of leaders over the last ten years I rarely hear love mentioned. Yet love is why we choose to lead in the first place. This might sound overly generous with people's motivations, but if our purpose is to allow people to understand and solve their own problems, then it must be the primary motivation. It might help to consider it in the negative: what is leadership if it does not contain any love? Is it still leadership? It might be managing, being an entrepreneur, dictating or manipulating, things that are more focused on ourselves and our needs alone rather than the wellbeing of all of us.

Without love as a guiding force in leadership it is easy to get lost—when things get hard, when our motivation waivers, when we get caught up in ourselves and our factions. Love helps us remember our purpose and who we are really serving. Without love we can also miss many important things along the way—what people are feeling, how they experience us and whether they are more free than when they started. Love is the unifying force for all the other practices, ideas and reflections in this book.

Maybe our problem with talking about love in leadership is the skewed idea we have of love. Popular culture portrays love mostly as what the Ancient Greeks called *eros* (passionate, sensual love), *philia* (friendship and bonding) and *storge* (the affection most often felt by parents for their children). Two other types of love, *agape* and *pragma*, are less often talked about. *Agape* is selfless, divine, non-romantic love. *Pragma* is a more practical, realistic and mutually beneficial love (one can often see this kind of love between old married couples). These two last types of love, I think, are at the core of leadership—useful leadership.

Perhaps if we can move away from the 'romance', or what I have earlier described as the 'fantasy', of leadership we can see a deeper and lasting way of approaching the idea of love in leadership, one that requires a love that won't falter or fade. Maybe that will allow us to see how love and leadership are actually woven together.

ONE AND THE SAME

So far it seems the idea of leadership and love being linked has been some kind of secret or embarrassing truth. But it is, in fact, staring us in the face. When we move beyond the idea of leadership as 'getting people to do stuff for you' then we see that leadership and love are actually one and the same.

Leading like loving:

. . . *is something we do.* We don't 'have' leadership or love. It is only real when it is in use.

. . . *requires others.* Leadership is not a solo sport. If we are alone, we are not leading any more. Similarly, in love, it only means something with others.

. . . *takes us beyond concern for ourselves.* We have all had alleged leaders who were only interested in themselves.

Similarly, we have had lovers who were the same. Maybe we have been that lover. To last, love and leadership means thinking of others.

... *requires us to give to be able to get.* We end up being the biggest winners when we are able to give. Giving is also getting.

... *requires risk.* Making ourselves vulnerable, speaking the unspeakable, doing what we haven't done before are necessary and rewarding.

... *explains the risk.* Why else would we take the risk of pain, rejection, loss, loneliness, marginalisation and confusion if we didn't care about those we love and lead?

... *needs conflict to grow.* Our differences hold wisdom and energy. Systems and relationships grow and become stronger in their ability to use conflict productively.

... *entails loss and failure.* For things to grow there is also loss. In our personal lives and our work, when we move from one place to another there are some things we need to leave behind. Sometimes we have no choice—they are taken from us.

... *has no boundaries.* Where we come from, what our profession is and what level we are at makes no difference. Everyone, everywhere has the opportunity to lead and love.

... *has no experts.* We can learn from others but ultimately we have to find our own way to love and lead in our context. These are our single greatest opportunities to be creative and unique in our lives from wherever we are.

... *can make us cynical, anxious or scared.* Our bad experiences can harden and close us. It can feel counterintuitive to continue opening ourselves up. It may seem more natural to be fearful and cynical ... and alone.

. . . requires us to hold steady. It will not be all rainbows and singing every day. It is often hard work and requires persistence, discipline and patience. We may forget why we started.

. . . means we have to be ready to be wrong. This is part of the process and growth required in us, not just those we love and lead.

If we can start to see how linked leadership and love are, then this allows us to change the question of what is required in the work we do. In addition to thinking 'what leadership is required here', what would happen if we thought 'what love is required here'? Does this change the relationship and idea we have to the challenges we face? Does it give us a stronger base to work from and simultaneously more freedom? It will certainly give us a more mature idea of leadership—beyond romance and kindness—to ensure that people can grow (even when that means we need to be 'tough').

BRINGING FREEDOM

There is a term that has appeared in the organisational development field in the last few years: 'discretionary effort'. This is the effort that employees are capable of bringing to their work beyond the minimum that is required. In some organisations finding ways to tap into this effort has become the holy grail of employee engagement and performance improvement. Organisations look for the formula of finding and tapping this effort due to the benefits it brings of higher productivity, lower staff turnover, higher innovation and better customer satisfaction. Yet it appears in our personal lives all the time.

In our loving relationships we seem capable of things we never thought possible when we only had ourselves to look after: staying up talking all night with a lover, going to work after a night of sleepless or sick children, carrying on after death and loss, cleaning up our children's vomit, helping out in the kids' canteen or football team after hours for no pay. We are capable of tremendous energy, perseverance and resilience in our love lives. Without this 'discretionary effort' families wouldn't work, our love lives wouldn't work, our friendships wouldn't work, our communities wouldn't work. Indeed every day we see the consequences when this discretionary effort is *not* expended: on our streets and schools, in our gaols and on our televisions.

Similarly in leading, out of love, we put in the discretionary effort we believe is necessary to make our community, organisation or country better.

But our aim is the same whether we are parents, leading organisational change or advocating for human rights. To paraphrase the singer Sting, if we love someone our aim is to 'set them free'. If we can free our spouses, children, co-workers, employees and community members they can solve their own problems and lead happier, more fulfilled lives.

This book has tried to look more deeply into the personal, inner challenges we face if we aim to bring this freedom. To do this I have proposed that we need to:

Grow out of the fantasies that other people will solve our problems or that we can solve other people's problems without us working together. We have to fail the expectation of being the 'hero' leader or pleasing people.

Step into our authority power by understanding its importance and limitations. Our challenge is to let go of control and step into our responsibility. When we do this we step into the mire of people's expectations and narratives and ultimately have to artfully fail if we wish to succeed. We need to step forward and let go at the same time.

Get some skin in the game and acknowledge that we have to change too. Inevitability we are part of the problem we are trying to fix. If we are not, then we can't be a part of finding a solution; we remain in our comfort zone while we expect others to do all the uncomfortable work.

Find a new relationship to compassion to move away from pride, pity and an attachment to compassion on our terms. We can practise compassion based on creativity, listening and trust rather than our personal desires to maintain control or fix people.

Bring wisdom to leading rather than judgement. Our judgements bring us certainty. Yet part of the creative process of leadership involves disequilibrium and uncertainty. If we can live without the certainty of our judgements for a little while we can find new partners, spaces and conversations that will uncover the wisdom inside the system.

Be generous with our passion and side with the whole—not just our faction, point of view or ideology. Practising and seeking even small moments of neutrality allow our love to be brought to everyone and bring fluidity to stuck problems.

Recognise the inevitability of betrayal in making progress. Benefiting the whole means that we often betray those who have supported us or we may betray some of our own needs. Surviving the backlash of not giving the system what it wants in the short term is an expression of love, not cruelty.

Understand collaboration (or solving problems together) is hard because we don't know how to be incompetent. We have been successfully taught to work alone or for our own interests. No one has taught us how to work together across difference. Our incompetence makes us vulnerable, yet vulnerability can give us strength.

Bring joy into leading and loving or no one is going to follow. If we can be grateful for the opportunity to lead and learn, we can show others that it might be worth coming along . . . or leading themselves.

Learn to live with and learn from hopelessness rather than just trading in hope. Hopelessness can teach us about being present and acceptance: to overcome and the temptation to just do something because we can't bear the uncertainty and difficulty. Hopelessness teaches us about something more sustainable than hope: love.

CONTINUING THE (LOVE) STORY

When we move past the romance we face the reality of making love work. The drudgery, the hard work, the repetition, the lack of time for ourselves. If you have children you know that there is lots of hard work. There are expectations on you, we have roles to play, there is a lot of mundane routine work to be done, you get blamed for other people's problems and there are messes to clean up—yours and others. It's the same to lead.

And there are amazing moments of joy and love that are what keep us going. Usually we are shown these moments through others. Through our children and their experiences of the world: their amazement, curiosity, energy and absolute focus on the moment. Childhood has a good reputation for a reason! Through our partner when we make love, when they surprise us, through their generosity and thoughtfulness. Through our colleagues, supporters and subordinates when they grow, learn, help each other and step up and lead.

These friends, helpers, enemies, family and lovers are all part of one larger leadership story in which we are just a player attempting to make progress. It is a story that began before us and will continue after we are gone. Like love there is no end and no winning in leadership. Those we work with—our friends, foes, partners and helpers—are like our lovers, children and spouses; they may not get better or worse: they just are. Our task is to engage in a constant act of generosity with ourselves and them. Sometimes we are wise, compassionate and helpful and sometimes we are not. It is the same for them. All the time we seek a constant deepening, uncovering and understanding of potential. We have the opportunity to repay the gift that has been given to us by allowing others to lead.

My hope in this book has been to break down some of the fantasies about leadership: that leaders will save us, fix our problems and make us feel good. Or that in leadership we just need passion and commitment; that we need to fight for our cause and that we won't have losses on our own side. That it's all about hope and glory. That compassion is just about being kind. That our power and love should be hidden. I have tried to promote what I think is the inner work of useful leadership—the kind of inner work that can have outer meaning. That goes beyond good intentions.

If I could challenge one last thing in this book, it is that leadership and love have little or nothing to do with each other. This is the final integration in my experience and brings us to where our work is—in leading just like in love—right here and now. Here and now is where courage is required.

We often think of the leaders we admire as exhibiting great courage. I think what they exhibit is love. Love takes courage. It takes courage to love enough to push ourselves into places where we might be wrong, might be disliked and are uncertain about the outcomes. It takes courage to love enough that we are willing to let go of the protection.

But most of all it takes courage to love enough to step into the full potential of who we are: our compassion, wisdom, power and rank, head and heart—all our imperfections and strengths together. This kind of love makes us really stretch to understand what is being asked of us right now. We are being called from the future to continue the story of leading and loving.

I wish you luck, and love, in your leadership.

Further reading

Chödrön, Pema, *When Things Fall Apart*, Element Publishing, London, 1997.

Heifetz, Ronald & Linsky, Marty, *Leadership on the Line*, Harvard Business School Press, Boston, 2002.

Mindell, Arnold, *The Year One*, Penguin, London, 1989.

Nydahl, Ole, *The Way Things Are*, Blue Dolphin Publishing, California, 1996.

Obama, Barack, *Dreams of my Father*, Crown Publishing Group, New York, 1995.

—— *The Audacity of Hope: Thoughts on Reclaiming the American Dream*, Crown Publishing Group, New York, 2006.

ON COLLABORATION

Austin, James E., *The Collaboration Challenge*, Jossey-Bass, New Jersey, 2000.

Kahane, Adam, *Solving Tough Problems*, Berrett-Koehler Publishers, San Francisco, 2007.

Lewis, Myrna & Woodhull, Jennifer, *Inside the No, Five Steps to Decisions That Last*, 2008.

Mindell, Arnold, *The Leader as Martial Artist*, Lao Tse Press, Portland, Oregon, 2000.

Notes

CHAPTER 1   LEADERSHIP FANTASIES

1   Beer, M. & Nohria, N., 'Cracking the code of change', *Harvard Business Review*, Vol. 78, No. 3, 2000.

2   Ashkenas, R.N. & Francis, S.C., 'Integration managers: special leaders for special times', *Harvard Business Review*, Vol. 78, No. 6, 2000.

3   Arthur D. Little, Consulting Survey on Change Success Rates, 2002.

4   Heifetz, Ronald, *Leadership Without Easy Answers*, Harvard University Press, Boston, 1994.

5   ibid.

6   Kahane, A., *Solving Tough Problems*, Berrett-Koehler Publishers, San Francisco, 2004.

7   Bennett, D., 'Perfectly happy', *The Boston Globe*, May 10, 2009.

CHAPTER 2   AUTHORITY AND FREEDOM

1   Sroufe, L.A., 'The role of infant-caregiver attachment in development', in Belsky, J. & Nezworski, T. (eds.), *Clinical Implications of Attachment*, Erlbaum, Hillsdale, NJ, 1988, pp. 18–38.

2   Fox, N.A., 'Temperament and regulation of emotion

in the first years of life', *Pediatrics*, Vol. 102, No. 5, pp. 1230–34, November 1998.

3 Obama, Barack, *Dreams From My Father*, Crown Publishing Group, New York, 1995.

4 Heifetz, R. & Laurie, D., 'Mobilizing adaptive work—beyond visionary leadership', chapter 3 of *The Leaders Change Handbook: An Essential Guide to Setting Direction and Taking Action*, Jossey-Bass, San Francisco, 1998.

5 McLean, B. & Elkind, P., *The Smartest Guys in the Room: The Amazing Rise and Scandalous Fall of Enron*, Portfolio, New York, 2004.

6 Oglensky, Bonnie D., 'Socio-psychoanalytic perspectives on the subordinate', *Human Relations*, New York, Vol. 48, Iss. 9, September 1995.

7 ibid.

8 Yiannis, G., 'Meeting god: when organizational members come face to face with the supreme leader', *Human Relations*, Vol. 50, No. 4, Springer, April 1997.

9 Hirschhorn & Bennis (1989) quoted in G. Yiannis ibid.

10 Freud (1959) quoted in G. Yiannis op. cit.

CHAPTER 3   ADAPTATION

1 Kegan, R. & Laskaw Lahey, L., *Immunity to Change: How to Overcome It and Unlock the Potential in Yourself and Your Organization*, Harvard Business School Publishing Corporation, Boston, 2009.

2 McLean, B. & Elkind, P., *The Smartest Guys in the Room: The Amazing Rise and Scandalous Fall of Enron*, Portfolio, New York, 2004.

CHAPTER 4   POWER AND COMPASSION

1   Boyatzis, R.E., Smith, M. & Blaize, N., 'Developing sustainable leaders through coaching and comparison', *Academy of Management Journal on Learning and Education*, 5(1), pp. 8–24.

2   Interview with Collette Livermore, *Following Mother Teresa*, ABC Radio National, 23 November 2008.

3   Trungpa, Chögyam, *The Collected Works of Chögyam Trungpa—Volume Six*, Shambhala, Boston, 2004.

4   Chödrön, Pema, *When Things Fall Apart*, Element Publishing, London, 1997.

CHAPTER 5   WISDOM NOT JUDGEMENT

1   Wheatley, Margaret J., *Leadership and the New Science*, Berrett W Koehler, San Francisco, 1992.

CHAPTER 6   NEUTRALITY AND PASSION

1   Carlin, Tony, *Playing With the Enemy: Nelson Mandela and the Game That Made a Nation*, Atlantic Books, London, 2008.

2   Mindell, Arnold, *The Year One*, Penguin, London, 1989.

3   'Pandora', Encyclopedia Mythica from Encyclopedia Mythica Online, http://www.pantheon.org/articles/p/pandora.html, accessed 30 March 2010.

CHAPTER 7   BETRAYAL, TRUST AND IDENTITY

1   Toynbee, Arnold, *Larousse Encyclopedia of Ancient and Medieval History*, Hamlyn Publishing, London, 1965.

2   Krantz, James, *Leadership, Betrayal and Adaptation*, The
    Tavistock Institute, SAGE Publications, London, 2006.

3   Heifetz, Ronald, *Leadership Without Easy Answers*,
    Harvard University Press, Boston, 1994.

4   Krantz, James, op. cit.

5   Dworkin, Jan & Menken, Dawn, presentation at the
    Worldwork Conference, London, 2008.

6   Chödrön, Pema, *The Places that Scare You*, Element
    Publishing, London, 2001.

CHAPTER 8   COLLABORATION, INCOMPETENCE AND VULNERABILITY

1   Perlow, Leslie, *When You Say Yes But Mean No. Finding
    Support and Supporting Others*, Crown Business
    Publishing, New York, 2003.

2   Argyris, Chris, 'Teaching smart people how to learn',
    Harvard Business Review, Boston, May–June 1991.

3   Brim, Gilbert, *Ambition: How We Manage Success and
    Failure Throughout Our Lives*, Basic Books, New York,
    1992.

CHAPTER 9   JOY, GRATITUDE AND INSPIRATION

1   Coady, Tony, as quoted in 'Why it doesn't hurt to say
    thank you', *Sydney Morning Herald*, April 2, 2010.

CHAPTER 10   THE TEACHER IN HOPELESSNESS

1   Grayling, A.C., *The Meaning of Things: Applying Phil-
    osophy to Life*, Weidenfeld & Nicholson, London, 2001.

2 Chödrön, Pema, *The Places That Scare You: A Guide to Fearlessness in Difficult Times*, Element Publishing, London, 2001.

3 Singer, Peter, *How Are We To Live: Ethics In An Age of Self-interest*, Prometheus Books, New York, 1995.

Index